Edinburgh
Hidden Walks

Alan Sharp

Published by Geographers'
A-Z Map Company Limited
An imprint of HarperCollins Publishers
Westerhill Road
Bishopbriggs
Glasgow
G64 2QT

HarperCollinsPublishers
1st Floor, Watermarque Building,
Ringsend Road, Dublin 4, Ireland

www.az.co.uk
a-z.maps@harpercollins.co.uk

1st edition 2022

A catalogue record for this book
is available from the British Library.

ISBN 978-0-00-849631-9

10 9 8 7 6 5 4 3 2 1

Printed in the UK

MIX
Paper from
responsible sources
FSC www.fsc.org **FSC™ C007454**

contents

introduction

When you think of Edinburgh, you think of the castle on a rock, the Royal Mile sweeping downwards towards Holyrood Palace and the narrow closes falling away on either side. For eleven months of the year, this street is teeming with tourists, buying kilts and shortbread and snapping photos of everything that moves or stands still. Then each August it plays host to the Fringe, the world's most popular open arts festival and you can barely move without someone trying to convince you that their show is the one you need to see.

But Edinburgh is truly one of the great capital cities of Europe, and there is so much more to see than just the Old Town area. Wander past Princes Street Gardens into the Georgian splendour of the New Town, explore the harbour fronts on the Forth Coast or take a leisurely riverside stroll along the Water of Leith.

The north of the city is a walker's paradise with a network of footpaths following the lines of the old industrial railways. To the west is South Queensferry with magnificent views of the famous Forth Bridges. To the east you can walk along the beach at Portobello or enjoy a pint in a historic pub frequented by Mary, Queen of Scots. And to the south, great houses and dramatic landscapes await.

If you thought you knew Edinburgh, then my hope is that by following the walks in this book, you will discover that you have only just scraped the surface.

about the author

Alan Sharp is a professional tour guide, conducting historical walking tours in York and Edinburgh, and is the proprietor of White Rose York Tours. He has written books and magazine articles on the subjects of history, true crime and mountaineering. He lives in York and has three grown-up children.

how to use this book

Each of the 20 walks in this guide is set out in a similar way. They are all introduced with a brief description, including notes on things you will encounter on your walk, and a photograph of a place of interest you might pass along the way.

On the first page of each walk there is a panel of information outlining the distance of the walk, a guide to the walking time, and a brief description of the path conditions or the terrain you will encounter. A suggested starting point along with the nearest postcode is shown, although postcodes can cover a large area therefore this is just a rough guide.

The major part of each section is taken up with route maps and detailed point-to-point directions for the walk. The route instructions are prefixed by a number in a circle, and the corresponding location is shown on the map.

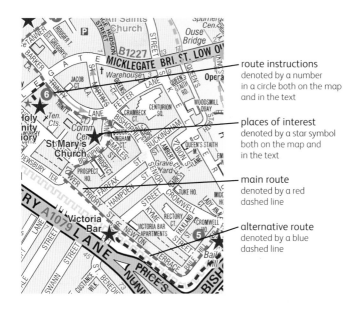

route instructions
denoted by a number in a circle both on the map and in the text

places of interest
denoted by a star symbol both on the map and in the text

main route
denoted by a red dashed line

alternative route
denoted by a blue dashed line

⒜⒵ walk one

Old Town Memorials

Greyfriars Kirkyard and the Vennel.

If you have ever perused the postcards in an Edinburgh tourist shop, you will have seen views of Edinburgh Castle from the Vennel, and maybe spent time trying to work out where the photographs were taken from. This walk takes you to this spot, as well as some of the other lesser-known sights of the Old Town away from the Royal Mile.

Greyfriars Kirkyard is best known for Bobby, the faithful dog who attended his master's grave every day. A statue of him stands across the road from the main entrance. But also here you will find the doggerel poet William MacGonagall, William Smellie, the man responsible for the Encyclopedia Britannica, and Thomas Riddel whose name may or may not have inspired a character in the Harry Potter books.

The walk also includes a wander around George Square, at the heart of Edinburgh University. Laid out in the Georgian period, it features a secluded garden where the students can study or socialize in peace on sunny days. The walk starts and ends at the Usher Hall, Edinburgh's premier classical concert venue built in 1914 in an unusual circular domed style.

start / finish	Usher Hall, Lothian Road
nearest postcode	EH1 2EA
distance	2½ miles / 4 km
time	1 hour
terrain	Surfaced roads, uneven graveyard paths, some steps and steep hills.

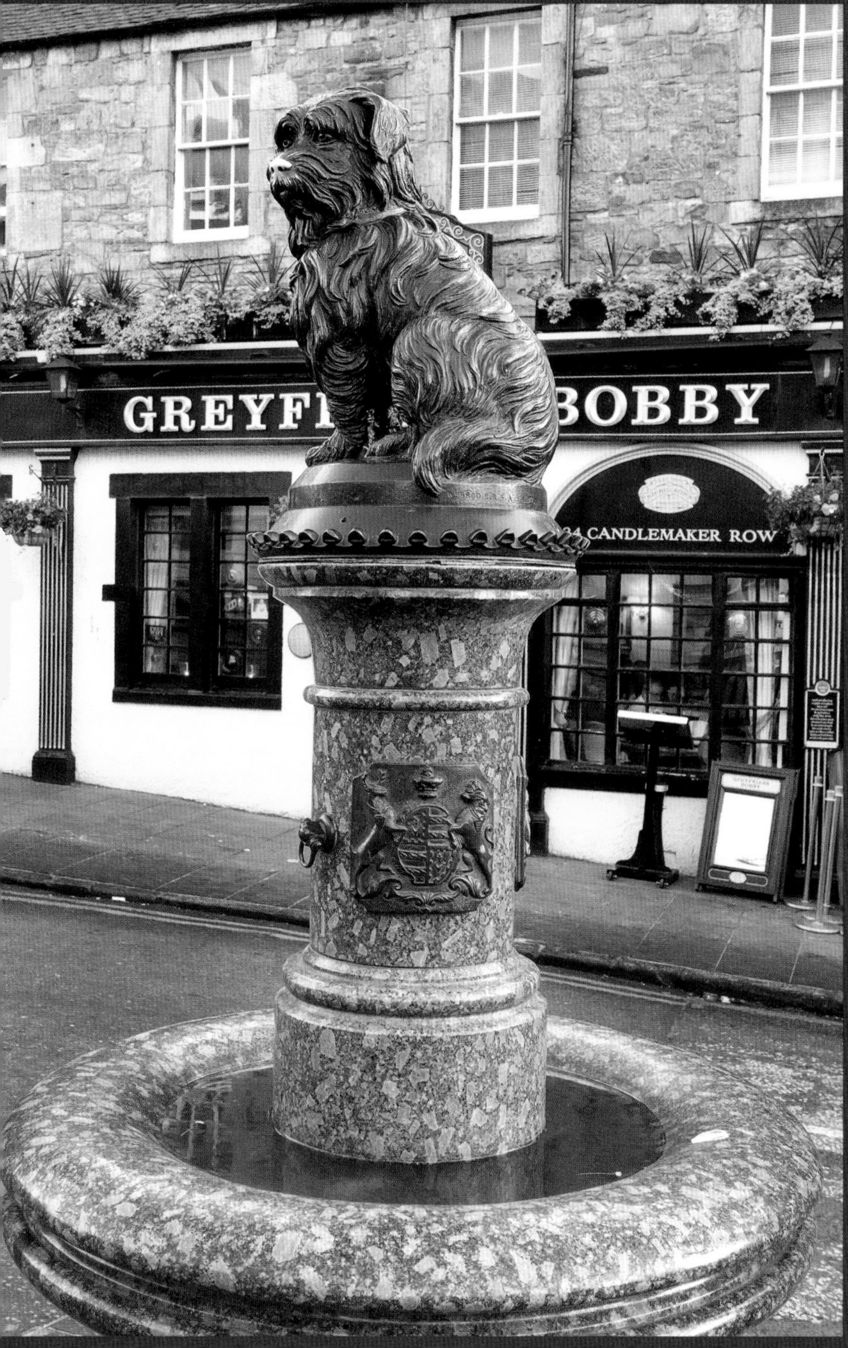
GREYF
BOBBY
34 CANDLEMAKER ROW

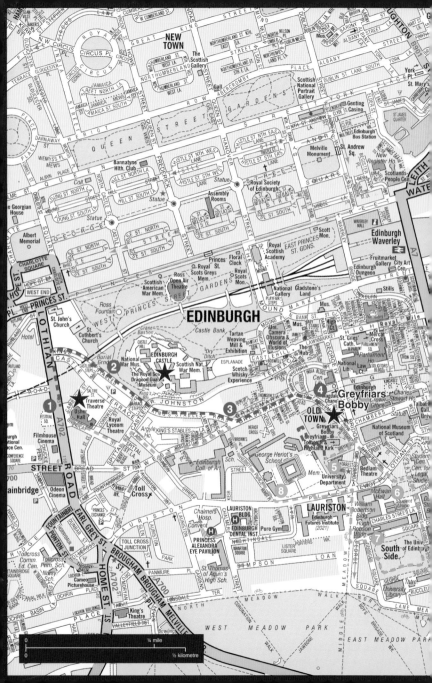

1 From the front steps of the Usher Hall, head forward and right to the corner of Shakespeares pub, and walk down Lothian Road. At the next corner you will notice there are two roads next to each other leading to the right, the first sloping upwards and the second slightly downwards. Cross the first using the pedestrian crossing, and turn right into the second, King's Stables Road.

2 As you pass along this road, just before you reach the pedestrian entrance to the multi-storey car park on the right, you will see a side entrance to Princes Street Gardens on your left. Have a quick look inside the entrance and you will see the little-known statue of Bum the Vagabond Dog, on the ground on the left-hand side. Bum was a dog who survived on the streets of San Diego, California, by the goodwill of the people, and because of the similarity to Edinburgh's Greyfriars Bobby story, the two cities exchanged replicas of their respective statues in 2008. Continue along King's Stables Road, passing under a road bridge, until you reach the Grassmarket.

3 Turn left into the Grassmarket and walk through it, moving in a more-or-less diagonal direction as you want to reach the right-hand corner on the opposite end. Here you will find a road called Cowgatehead, which leads to a mini roundabout. At this you want to take the road to the right, and just a few yards along you will see an arched gate in the wall on your right.

4 Go through this gate and up the steps and you are in the Greyfriars Kirkyard. You can wander here as much as you want, but to see most of the well-known graves, take the following route:

Head towards the church, then take the fork on the left which will lead you past the grave of John Grey, Bobby's owner. Once you are level with the church, turn right and pass on its right-hand side. At the end of the church, go straight and you will see an arch in the wall. Go through and turn immediately right, which will lead you down to the grave of Thomas Riddel. At the bottom, go left and left again and walk up the opposite side of the enclosure you are in. At the top there is a set of gates into the grounds of George Heriot's School on the right and in front of you is a plaque on the wall commemorating William MacGonagall.

Turn left again and return through the arch, then turn right and towards the top of this path you pass the grave of William Smellie. In front of you are the gates of the Covenanters Prison. In the small enclosure on the other side, over 1,000 Covenanter prisoners, captured at the Battle of Bothwell Brig in 1679, were held and many died from exposure or ill treatment. Turn left and as you walk along here you pass the imposing Mackenzie mausoleum, last resting place of George Mackenzie, the man who ordered them to be detained there. It is said to be haunted by his spirit.

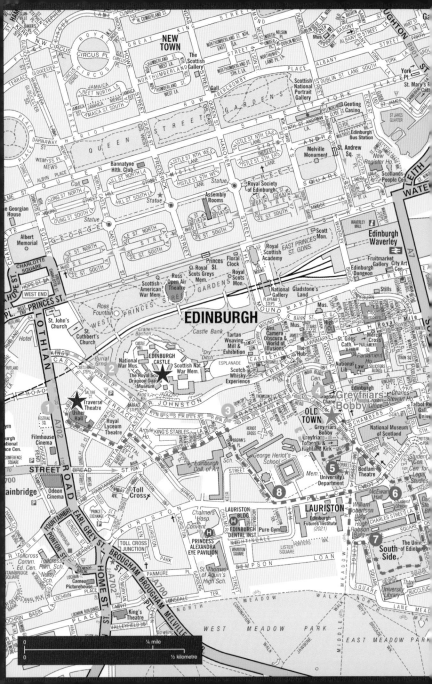

5 Turn left again to reach the main entrance of the kirkyard. There is a gravestone here dedicated to Greyfriars Bobby, although it is unlikely he was actually laid to rest here. As you exit the graveyard you will see Bobby's statue ★ across the road. However, turn right and walk up the street to where the road forks either side of the Bedlam Theatre. Take the left fork, and continue to the end of this road, crossing over to the open area of Bristo Square.

6 Cross the square diagonally to the left, and take the path that runs alongside the modern university buildings and shortly becomes Charles Street. Continue straight ahead into George Square, and halfway down the square on your right you will see a gate into the gardens. Go through and take paths to cross to the opposite side of the gardens where you will find another gate to exit by. Then turn right.

7 Once you return to the top of George Square, turn left into George Square Lane and keep going straight until you reach a foot and cycle path called Middle Meadow Lane. Turn right and keep going until you reach the road. Turn left at the road and you will notice you are passing George Heriot's School on the right. Just before you get to the main entrance of the school there is a pedestrian crossing, cross over here and continue along the road. At the end of the school grounds there is a turning on the right into Heriot Place.

8 Take this turning and continue until the road becomes the Vennel and descends a series of steps. From the top here you will get that magnificent view of Edinburgh Castle ★ . At the bottom of the steps you are back at the Grassmarket. Turn left and head up the West Port. Continue until you reach a main crossroads, then turn right into Lady Lawson Street. At the end, turn left and immediately right and you will be in Grindlay Street. At the end of this you return to the Usher Hall.

AZ walk two

National Monuments

Calton Hill and the Stones of Scotland.

We start this walk at the Balmoral Hotel, whose clock tower is one of Edinburgh's most instantly recognized landmarks. The clock is always set 3 minutes fast so that people heading for nearby Waverley Station are early for their trains.

A walk across Calton Hill includes many well-known sights including the unfinished National Monument, originally intended as a replica of the Parthenon in Athens. Also on the hill are the Nelson and Dugald Stewart monuments, the Playfair Observatory and the Portuguese cannon. As we come down from the hill we pass a beacon commemorating a vigil held on this spot for five years during the 1990s by supporters of a devolved Scottish parliament.

In the same vein, we visit the Stones of Scotland. This sculpture was created in 2002 to celebrate the intended opening date of the new parliament building. Taking the form of a stone circle, it includes one stone from each of the 32 council areas of Scotland.

We also pass Queen Mary's Bath House. This intriguing 16th-century building stands at the edge of the grounds of Holyrood Palace and is associated with Mary, Queen of Scots, although it is unlikely she ever bathed there.

start / finish	Balmoral Hotel, Princes Street
nearest postcode	EH2 2EQ
distance	2¼ miles / 3.7 km
time	1 hour
terrain	Surfaced roads and paths, some steps and steep hills.

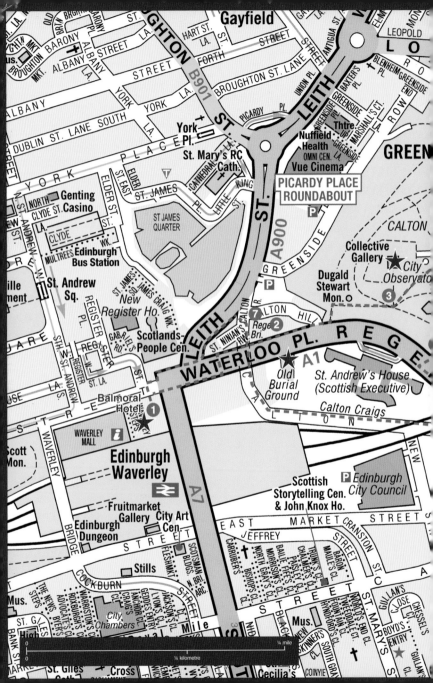

HILLSIDE CRESCENT

Bowling Green

BRUNTON

PLACE

EASTER

B1350

ROYAL-TERRACE GARDENS

L O N D O N   R O A D   G A R D E N S

NORTON PL.

ROAD

T E R R A C E   CARLTON

CARLTON TER.

CARLTON T. BRAE

EASTER

MONTROSE

KYLE PL.

CARLTON

CARLTON TER. MEWS

ROYAL TERRACE M.

REGENT T. MEWS

CARLTON TER. LA.

CARLTON TER.

Tennis Courts

R E G E N T

G A R D E N S

Stones of Scotland

Pav. Bowls

ABBEYMOUNT

CROFT-AN-RIGH

TYTLER

CALTON

T E R R A C E

ROAD

A1

REGENT PARK

⑤

ABBEYHILL

National Monument

Monument

R E G E N T

CRES.

Queen Mary's Bath House

Parliament House

ABBEYHILL

King Edward VII Mem.

Holyrood Ab (remains

Burns Monument

Calton New Burial Ground

⑥

★

Holyrood Pala

NETHER CRAIGWELL

CALTON HILL STAIRS

R O A D

THOMSON'S CT.

ABBEY STRAND

The Queen's Gallery

Pala Holyroo

WHITE HORSE CL.

ROBERT-SON'S CT.

HORSE WYND

CALTON WYND

LOCHEND CL.

CAMPBELL CL.

BROWN'S ENTRY

GALLOWAY'S CL.

Canon: Kirk Old

PANMURE CL.

DUNBAR'S CL.

BROWN'S CT.

REID'S CT.

REID'S CL.

Royal Mile Prim. Sch.

SHUTTON RD.

Scottish Parliament

QUEEN'S DR.

People's Story

Lib Bull's

CRICHTON'S CLOSE

JACKSON'S ENTRY

Mus.

SUGARHOUSE CL.

WILSON'S CT.

OLD TOLBOOTH WYND

GENTLES ENTRY

SLATER'S STEPS

BAKEHOUSE CLOSE

HAMMERMEN'S ENTRY

HOLYROOD ROAD

Dynamic Earth

University of Edinburgh

JOHN ST.

VIEWC

LOCHVIEW COURT

HOLYROOD GAIT

HOLYROOD

1 Beginning at the front steps of the Balmoral Hotel, turn right and head to the corner, then cross North Bridge at the pedestrian crossing. On the other side, continue along the road, and cross Waterloo Place at the next pedestrian crossing, although you might want to continue along on this side and pay a short visit to the Old Calton Burial Ground ★, whose entrance is on the right. It contains a monumental obelisk and the mausoleum of the philosopher David Hume. If you do decide to visit the graveyard, on exiting again find a safe place to cross to the other side of the road.

2 After crossing Waterloo Place, turn right and continue along until you see some stairs on the left signposted 'Nelson Monument'. Climb these stairs and then turn immediately right to climb the next long set of stairs. At the top of these, continue up the path climbing quite steeply. At the junction, turn and look behind you for the Dugald Stewart Monument. You can follow the path along to the left if you wish to visit it.

3 Otherwise, facing up the hill, take the left-hand fork of the path twice and you will find yourself walking to the left of the Portuguese cannon. Keep going until you reach the square in front of the National Monument ★, cross over to the opposite corner and take the narrow road that runs immediately to the left of the monument. Follow this as it runs downhill, curving round to the right around the foot of the hill, passing the commemorative beacon and continuing around to the right where the road runs back down to the exit of the hill.

4 On returning to the main road, cross carefully and turn left, then continue along Regent Road. You will pass the Burns Monument ★ and the entrance to the New Calton Burial Ground on your right, and then arrive at the gate to the Regent Road Park. Enter and turn left and follow the path alongside the road. Halfway along you will find the Stones of Scotland sculpture ★. Continue to the end of the park then turn right and right again to return along the other side.

5 Just before you return to the entrance, turn almost back on yourself to the left where there is another path descending the side of the hill. Follow this as it slopes on down until you reach a gate through to the road, then turn right. Carry on down the hill to where it levels off, passing Queen Mary's Bath House ★ on your left. Just after this, take the next turning on the right into Calton Road.

6 Walk up this road, keeping the wall of the New Calton Burial Ground on your right. You will pass a number of interesting mill buildings on your left. Further up, the buildings on the left become more modern, and then you pass the rear entrances to Waverley Station before the road curves round to the right and passes under a high bridge. Just after this, as you approach a junction, there are some steps on the left by the Black Bull pub.

7 Climb these steps and turn left to head uphill. At the junction with Waterloo Place, cross the road to your right using the pedestrian crossing, and pass the Wellington Statue on your right, then cross the road to the left using the next pedestrian crossing. Turn right to return to your start point.

AZ walk three

Parkland and Plague Pits

A walk around The Meadows.

The Old Town of Edinburgh is bounded on both sides by parkland. In the North is Princes Street Gardens, a popular spot for tourists and locals alike. To the south is The Meadows, a large expanse of open fields frequented by students from the nearby university, but often missed by visitors to the city.

Before we reach the park, our walk starts with the Old College of the University of Edinburgh, built in the late 18th century around a quadrangle where the University holds its graduation celebrations. Around the corner on Chambers Street is the National Museum of Scotland, the most visited tourist attraction in Scotland and considered one of the finest museums in the UK. It's free to enter and well worth a visit.

We then head to The Meadows where we take a circuit of this beautiful parkland. The paths here are lined with cherry trees so if you come in spring when they are in blossom, the sight is spectacular. As part of the walk we will pass through Bruntsfield Links, a short hole golf course where the locals practice the national obsession, little knowing that its bumps and hillocks are the result of it being laid out on the city's old plague pits where the victims of disease were buried.

Returning to the Old College we pass some nice churches and the city's Central Mosque, where the Mosque Kitchen is hugely popular with students for its cheap and filling vegetarian meals.

start / finish	Old College, University of Edinburgh, South Bridge
nearest postcode	EH8 9YL
distance	2¾ miles / 4.35 km
time	1 hour
terrain	Surfaced roads and pathways, moderate hills.

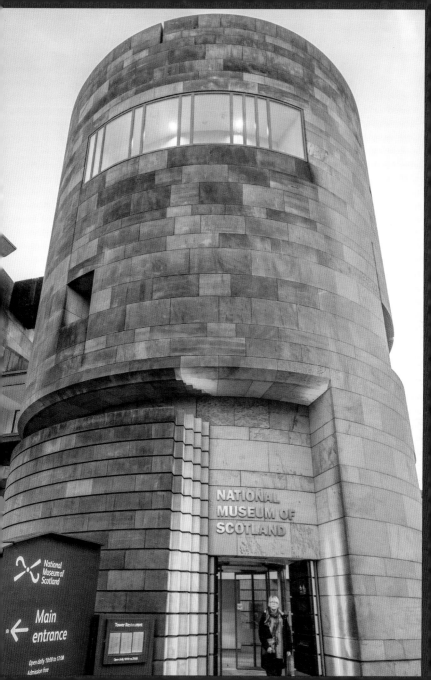

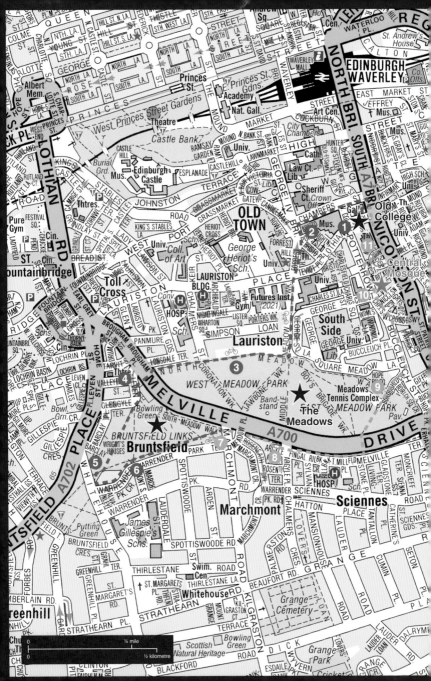

1 Depending on the time of day, begin the walk either in the quadrangle of the Old College ★ , or if the gates are closed then just outside. Exiting the college down the ramp through the main entrance, turn left onto South Bridge and then immediately left again onto Chambers Street. Follow this road past the old and then new buildings of the National Museum.

2 On the corner next to the turret-like entrance to the new building, turn left again, and when the road forks ahead of you take the right-hand fork into Forrest Road. At the end of this road, cross at the pedestrian crossing and go straight ahead into Middle Meadow Walk. At the bottom of the walk, footpaths lead away in five different directions across The Meadows ★ , but you need to turn right and take the one that leads along the edge of the parkland.

3 Keep following this path until you come to the road, where you will see the park entrance with its unicorn pillars to your right. There is a pedestrian and cycle crossing here, use this to cross the road and continue straight ahead on a path that has a hedge to one side and a short iron fence on the other.

4 This leads you to Leven Terrace, where you turn left and walk up the road until you reach the corner with the park once again ahead of you. Keep going straight onto the paved path here, and after a few yards take the path that forks away to the right. You are now crossing Bruntsfield Links ★ , site of the city's 17th-century plague pits and now a golf course, so be careful not to be hit by any stray golf balls.

5 At the top of this path, take the right-hand path and walk a short distance to the road, then turn left. Take the next left into Warrender Park Crescent. The impressive buildings on your left here are the former James Gillespie's High School, attended by Muriel Spark in the 1920s and said to be the inspiration for the school in her novel *The Prime of Miss Jean Brodie*.

6 Keep going around the crescent until you reach the park again. There is a pavement on the left of the road here, which shortly ends by veering to the left into the park. Follow this and then join the path that runs parallel to the buildings. Continue straight on this path until you reach another road.

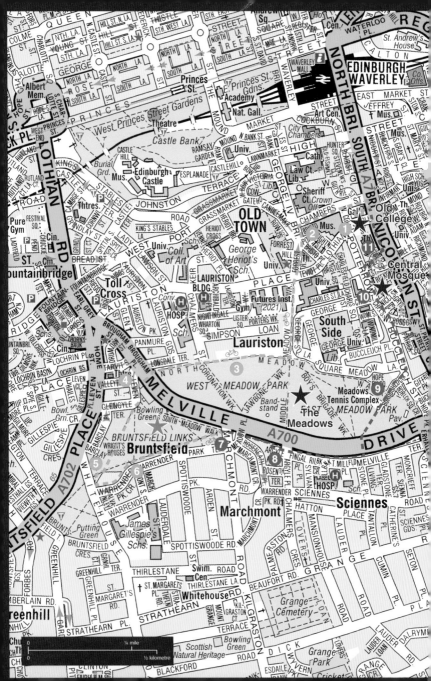

7 Cross using the pedestrian crossing, and follow the foot and cycle path slightly to the right crossing a short pedestrianized section of road and finding the foot and cycle path again as it runs parallel to the main road separated by a strip of grass and trees.

8 Continue along this until you reach the junction to Argyll Place. Cross this carefully and continue along the path on the other side. When you reach a pedestrian crossing with a fingerpost signed City Centre and George Square, turn left to cross the road and take the right-hand one of the three footpaths that lead across the park on the other side.

9 At the other end of this path you will see a gap between the buildings with some metal bollards, and the road name Boroughloch. Go through this gap and follow the narrow lane as it turns slightly left then right and joins Buccleuch Street (pronounced Buck-Loo). Continue left, passing the mid-19th-century Buccleuch Free Church on your right, and St Andrews Orthodox Church opposite it on the left.

10 Further along you will come to the modern university buildings and the Central Mosque ★. Take the first turning on the right after the mosque, into Marshall Street. After a very short distance the road forks to pass around Nicolson Square Gardens. Take the left-hand side and when you reach Nicolson Street, turn left onto it.

11 As you walk down the road you will pass the glass front of the Festival Theatre on your left, and the Surgeon's Hall Museum, which is well worth a visit, on your right. Cross the next junction and you will return to the front of the Old College.

A·Z walk four

Riverside Reflection

The Water of Leith and the West End.

Many people who visit Edinburgh stick to the Royal Mile and the wide streets of the New Town, never realizing that just a short distance away is one of the most beautiful spectacles of the city. The Water of Leith runs through a deep valley just north of the New Town, winding its way over rocks and waterfalls while picturesque houses cling to the steep valley walls above.

This walk takes in the most scenic stretch of the river, as well as passing by one of the statues in Antony Gormley's 6 TIMES series, standing in a deep pool above a weir. The walk also passes the Scottish National Gallery of Modern Art, which is well worth a visit if you pass during opening hours.

After leaving the riverside, the walk brings us back through the streets of the West End, where we encounter Edinburgh's second cathedral. Most visitors are familiar with St Giles on the Royal Mile, but the Episcopal Cathedral of St Mary, hidden away from the tourist trail, is every bit as magnificent. Built in the late 19th century in the gothic style, it features a 295-foot (90-metre) central spire and two further spires on the west end, and is the tallest building in the city.

start / finish	Haymarket Railway Station
nearest postcode	EH12 5EY
distance	4 miles / 6.4 km
time	1 hour 30 minutes
terrain	Surfaced roads, uneven riverside paths, some steps and steep hills.

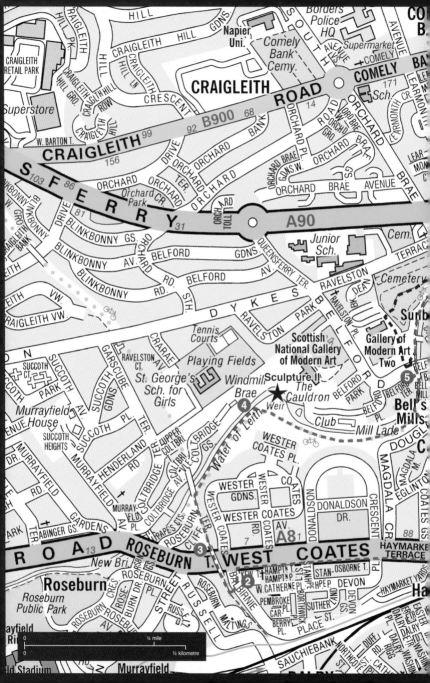

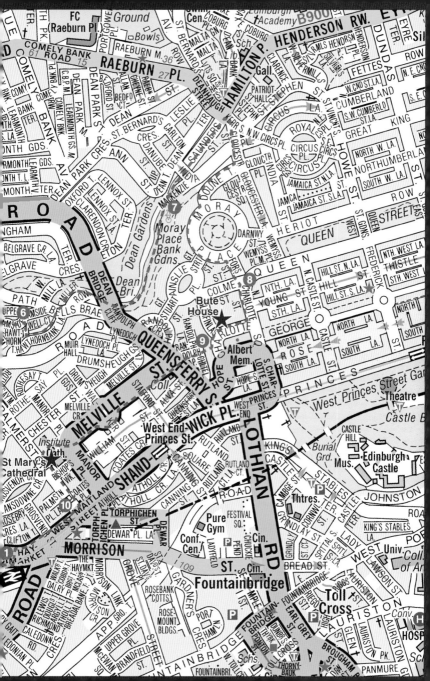

1 From the front of Haymarket Station, turn left and head along the road past the tram stop. On the right of the street a row of shops ends, and you will see the former Donaldson's School, a rather splendid building in the Jacobean style designed by William Playfair in 1851. Now being developed into residential accommodation, it was briefly considered as a potential home for the Scottish Parliament.

2 Continue along the road until, just after you pass a former church now housing the Scottish Bible Society, you see a bridge crossing the road. Just before this, a fingerpost pointing left indicates a foot and cycle path to Queensferry, Leith, Granton and Crewe Toll. Turn left here, and at the end of the building on the right you will see a footpath leading away from the road to the right. Follow this up a short slope where it joins another footpath, and turn right to cross the bridge you saw previously. This is again signposted for Granton and Leith.

3 Once across the bridge, the path is enclosed by trees on both sides, and after a short distance, just before it crosses another high bridge, you will see a narrow set of steps descending to the river on your left. Go down these steps and at the bottom veer right to walk along the riverbank with the river on your left.

4 Keep following the riverside path. After a while you will see a wide pool leading to a weir, and at the top of this is Sculpture II ★ of the Antony Gormley *6 TIMES* installation. The river turns at this point, but continue to follow it round on the main path until it reaches a point where it crosses a small bridge to the other side of the river. Follow briefly on the other side until you pass under a bridge.

5 The route continues along the riverside path, with the river on your right. Alternatively, if you wish to visit the Scottish National Gallery of Modern Art, take the steps just on the other side of the bridge, which will lead you to it. If you decide to take this detour, at the end of your visit you can either return to the path they way you came, or at the rear of the gallery you will find a gate into the Dean Cemetery. Follow the path straight through the cemetery and out through the gates on the opposite side, then turn right and head down the hill. Halfway down on the right you will see an opening with a red sign advertising the Water of Leith Walkway. This leads to a narrow set of steps that take you back down onto the riverside path.

6 Shortly after rejoining the path, it crosses the river once again on another bridge. At the other side, the dedicated path ends and you are in Hawthornebank Lane. Follow this road to the left as it rises quite steeply away from the river and you reach a junction with Bells Brea bridge on the left. Cross straight over this junction into Miller Row and continue to follow the river. As the road passes under the Dean Bridge, there are some metal poles marking where the road ends and it becomes a footpath again.

7 At the next bridge there is a large grassy area with steps up to road level. Go underneath this bridge and join the road again, which is Saunders Street. At the end of this road there is another crossroads with a bridge on the left. Turn right here and head up Kerr Street. Take the first right onto Gloucester Street, and then the second right onto Doune Terrace. This will bring you to Moray Place, a large circular garden surrounded by high terraced housing. Follow this round on either side until you reach the road directly opposite the one you entered by, which is Forres Street, and exit by this route.

8 You will go steeply uphill, crossing Queen Street using the pedestrian crossing, and reach Charlotte Square. Turn right when you reach the square. You will now be walking past Bute House ★, the official residence of Scotland's First Minister. At the next corner, turn left, and walk a short distance down until just as you reach a large imposing building which is West Register House, you will see a footpath leading off to your right.

9 Go along this footpath, and at the other end turn left and immediately right into Randolph Place. At the end of this street, cross the road using the pedestrian crossing and go straight ahead into Melville Street. At this point you will have a magnificent view of St Mary's Cathedral ★ directly ahead of you at the other end of the street. Continue along the street and pass the cathedral on either side, although the right may be more interesting, and when you reach the other side turn left into Palmerston Place.

10 Follow this road down, and as it reaches Atholl Place at the end, use the pedestrian crossing to cross the road and turn to the right. Follow this road down as it becomes Clifton Terrace and merges with Haymarket Terrace. When you reach the corner, Haymarket Station is directly opposite you and can be reached using the pedestrian crossing.

A͟Z walk five

Secrets of the New Town

Georgian splendour north of the city centre.

Many visitors to Edinburgh's New Town do not venture beyond Princes Street, George Street and Queen Street, so the rest of this area provides some less-visited sights only a stone's throw from the city centre.

The New Town was purpose-built in response to the overcrowding of the medieval Old Town. Conditions in Edinburgh had become so bad that anyone with ambition quickly moved to London, and the city was losing its brightest and best. The solution was to build a new city, with wide airy streets and good quality houses where the well-to-do could live. Built mostly in the 18th and early 19th centuries on a grid system, the New Town became something of a model city.

The walk mostly takes you round the second stage New Town development, passing many of its secluded private gardens and residential crescents. Along the way we pass through Stockbridge, with its independent boutiques, artisan shops and small galleries. We also take in the Stockbridge Colonies, a row of narrow side streets lined with terraced housing. These were built in the late 19th century to provide quality, affordable housing for the city's working classes. Opposite is the Glenogle Swim Centre, a fine example of a fully restored Victorian swimming bath.

start / finish	Edinburgh Bus Station, St Andrew's Square entrance
nearest postcode	EH1 3DQ
distance	2¾ miles / 4.4 km
time	1 hour
terrain	Surfaced roads and pathways, some steep hills and steps.

1 With your back to the St Andrew's Square entrance of Edinburgh Bus Station, turn right and head down the hill towards Queen Street. Cross at the pedestrian crossing and go through the fencing on the other side (there are steps or a ramp) and onto Dublin Street. Continue downhill until the next corner on the left, then turn into Abercromby Place.

2 Keeping to the left-hand side of the road, you can walk along the edge of Queen Street Gardens. This series of three gardens covers 8 acres of the city and is only accessible by local residents, but you will get views through the fence and trees of the landscaped space within. Follow the line of the gardens, keeping the fence on your left and crossing two main roads as you continue along.

3 After the second of the cross streets, you are in Heriot Row, and towards the end of this stretch of garden you will see a street kiosk with a right turn into India Street opposite. Take this turning and head down the hill on the right-hand side of the road. Take the second turning on the right and you will find yourself entering the Royal Circus. You need to exit directly on the opposite side, so you can go either way at this point, but in either case cross one road and turn off the Circus at the next, into North East Circus Place.

4 At the end of this road, turn left onto St Vincent Street, and you will see the imposing St Stephen's Theatre ahead of you. Go to the left of this and follow St Stephen Street round until you are in the heart of Stockbridge. At the end of the road, turn right onto Kerr Street and keep going until you cross a bridge over the Water of Leith. At the other side of this bridge, a set of steps goes down to the river on your right.

5 Descend the steps and turn left onto the riverside path. Follow this along until it brings you up onto the next bridge, then turn right and cross the bridge back across the river. Follow the road round as it becomes Glenogle Road, which takes you past the Stockbridge Colonies on your left and the Victorian baths ★ on your right. This brings you out onto Brandon Terrace, where you turn left and follow the road down to the pedestrian crossing, then cross over using the traffic island with the clock.

6 Having crossed, head left and immediately round the corner to the right. In front of you is Canon Street, turning off just before a petrol station. Walk up here to where it meets Eyre Place, follow this briefly round to the right and then cross the road into Logan Street. This street is signposted with a footpath fingerpost directing you to Warriston, City Centre, Leith and Newhaven.

7 At the end of this road is an entrance to King George V Park. Enter the park and turn left along the footpath. When you reach an area with a circular bench in the middle, take the middle of the three paths ahead of you. It is signposted to the city centre. Follow this path as it ascends and curves to the left, at the top of which you will come out of a gate where a triangular junction ahead of you takes you into Scotland Street. This is signposted to the city centre and Meadows.

8 Follow Scotland Street as it ascends quite steeply, then when you reach Drummond Place with a park ahead of you, turn left and follow the curved end of the park round, crossing London Street until you reach Dublin Street. Turn left onto this road and continue heading uphill until you once again reach the barriers with Queen Street behind. Cross over to return to your starting point.

A–Z walk six

Moorings and Mansions

The Union Canal and Morningside.

The Union Canal runs from Edinburgh to Falkirk, where it joins up with the Forth and Clyde Canal at the Falkirk Wheel. It was opened in 1822 and runs right into the heart of the city, although because it runs behind buildings and away from the main streets, even some local residents have no idea it is there.

This walk begins by following the towpath of the canal, before taking a walk through Morningside and Bruntsfield to return to the start. Morningside is one of the most affluent areas of the city; many of the local 'celebrity' population live here including television stars and well-known authors. The walk passes a number of very impressive large houses.

Heading from Morningside into Bruntsfield, we also pass through Holy Corner. This junction of Morningside Road, Chamberlain Road and Colinton Road features a church on each of the four corners of the crossroads. Three of these churches are still active and the fourth is now the Eric Liddell Centre, a community hub named after the Olympic athlete of *Chariots of Fire* fame. He used to worship at what is now the Morningside United Church, which stands on the other side of Chamberlain Road.

start / finish	Corner of Lauriston Place and Earl Grey Street
nearest postcode	EH3 9AQ
distance	3¾ miles / 6.2 km
time	1 hour 30 minutes
terrain	Surfaced roads and pathways, moderately steep hill.

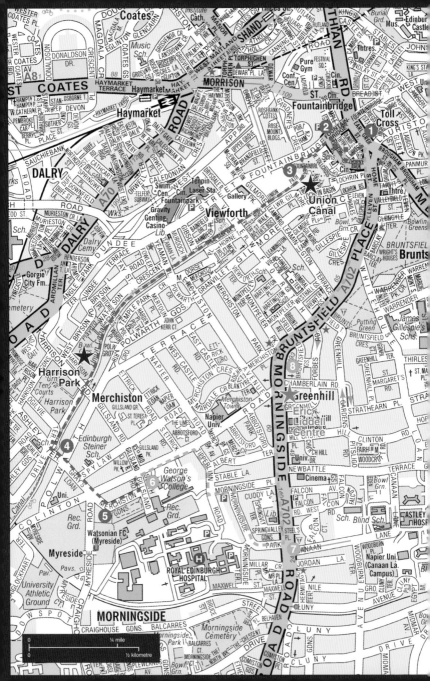

1 We begin the walk on the corner of Lauriston Place and Earl Grey Street, where there is a large open square in front of some modern buildings. From here, head across Earl Grey Street using the system of pedestrian crossings, then take the road straight ahead of you which is West Tollcross. At the corner by Tollcross fire station, turn right into Ponton Street and walk down to the end.

2 Now turn left into Fountainbridge and walk down around 50 yards (46 metres) where, just before a building with a curved front which is Companies House, you will see a narrow access road to your left with metal bollards on the end. Turn into this road and you will find yourself at the marina at the end of the Union Canal ★ .

3 Staying on the right-hand side of the canal, you will find the start of the towpath. Follow this for ¾ mile (1.2 km) passing three bridges, until you encounter Harrison Park ★ on your right. Pass beneath one more bridge, and then just before the next one you will see some steps up to a row of parked cars on your right.

4 Go up these steps onto Ogilvie Terrace, turn left and then left again to cross the bridge. You are now on Ashley Terrace. Continue straight across the next crossroads into Gray's Loan. Cross over Colinton Road, where there are two roads on the other side of the junction. Take the one that leads diagonally away to the left, which is Merchiston Gardens.

5 This road then curves away to the left, with views of the gardens themselves on your right, although this is a private garden, so there is no public access. When you reach the end of this road you will see the entrance to George Watson's College to your right, but turn left onto Gillsland Road, and then right at the end onto Colinton Road. There is a particularly impressive house on this corner.

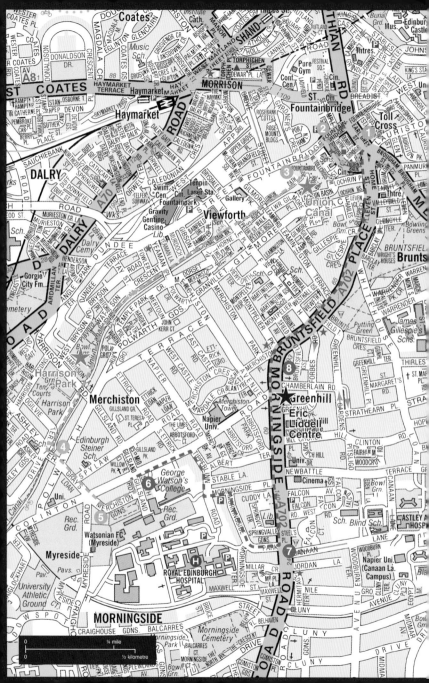

6 Continue along past George Watson's College, then take the next right into Tipperlinn Road. Follow this down, noting several mansion-like houses on your right, and take the third turning on the left into Morningside Place. Then turn first right into Morningside Park and follow this road as it curves away to the left and joins up with the main shopping street, Morningside Road.

7 Turn left onto this road and follow it as it climbs uphill, noting several nice independent cafés and boutiques among the shops here. If you want to stop for a coffee there are plenty of opportunities here. As you pass the end of the shops you will arrive at Holy Corner, where Colinton Road joins from the left and Chamberlain Road from the right. Continue straight across the junction where the road you are on now becomes Bruntsfield Place.

8 Continue on Bruntsfield Place as it curves to the right and begins to go downhill again. You will pass a large area of parkland on the right and shortly after that the King's Theatre. As you come to the foot of the slope you will see the Tollcross clock in the centre of the road and directly opposite on the diagonal is the square you started from. Use the pedestrian crossings to return to that point.

AZ walk seven

Ancient Landscape within the City

A trip around Arthur's Seat.

Many people visiting Edinburgh include a climb of Arthur's Seat on the itinerary, however a walk around the base of this extinct volcano can be just as rewarding. As you pass around the hill you will encounter several small lochs on which swans, geese and various wading birds congregate.

Also, while passing to the east, you may notice the faint step terracing which is evidence of crop cultivation when the hill was the home of the Votadini tribe, who began their occupation here around the early 5th century.

As we reach the rear of the hill, the walk descends to Duddingston. A historic but little-visited village, Bonnie Prince Charlie held a council of war here during the Jacobite rebellion, and Mary, Queen of Scots is said to have played skittles in the courtyard of the Sheep Heid Inn. We also circuit Duddingston Loch, used for skating and curling in centuries past, and the location of Henry Raeburn's famous *Skating Minister* painting which can be seen in the Scottish National Gallery in the city.

We return via the route of the former Edinburgh and Dalkeith Railway, known as the Innocent Railway due to it being horse-drawn, and finish with a walk to the west of the hill with magnificent views of Salisbury Crags.

start / finish	The Scottish Parliament building, Horse Wynd
nearest postcode	EH99 1SP
distance	5 miles / 8 km
time	2 hours
terrain	Surfaced roads and pathways, one dirt path, some steps and steep hills.

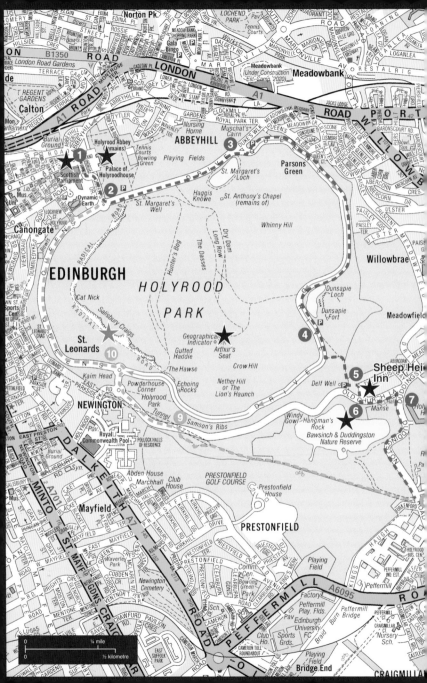

① Starting from the corner of the Royal Mile (Canongate) and Horse Wynd, with the Scottish Parliament ★ behind you and Holyrood Palace ★ in front, turn right and follow Horse Wynd as it turns first left then right and approaches Salisbury Crags, with a car park on your left. Continue to the roundabout and take the first (left) exit.

② When you reach the zebra crossing, cross over and continue to walk along to where the path forks with one path heading up Arthur's Seat ★. Take the left fork to continue along the side of the road. You will see the ruins of St Anthony's Chapel on the hillside to your right, and then you reach St Margaret's Loch.

③ Just past the loch a small road turns off to the right. Follow this road to continue on Queen's Drive, which now becomes a one track road with a footpath on the left. Continue on this path as it ascends quite steeply and passes Dunsapie Loch and its car park on your left.

④ After passing the car park, the road descends slightly and a hundred yards or so further it becomes fenced on the left. Just before the fence there is a bench for sitting, and in front of this a dirt path heads off to the left of the road down the hill. Follow this path, and it shortly joins a set of steps known as Jacob's Ladder. Continue down these steps to the bottom.

⑤ Just before you reach the road at the bottom, there is a pathway between the buildings on your left. Follow this path and you come out in front of the Sheep Heid Inn ★. You may want to break your journey with some refreshments or a game of skittles in the Victorian skittle alley here. Otherwise take the road to the right of the inn, which is The Causeway, and follow it to the end where you will see Duddingston Kirk on your right.

⑥ Turn left here along Old Church Lane, and when you reach the end turn right onto Duddingston Road West. Following this road you will notice the entrance to Dr Neil's Garden on your right. If you want a good view of Duddingston Loch ★, enter here and you can get right down to the waterside, then retrace your steps back to the road.

⑦ Follow the road along as it ascends until you see the entrance to Duddingston Golf Club on your left. Continue along through the more built-up area for 100 yards (91 metres) or so and you arrive at a pedestrian crossing. On your right there are turn-offs for a narrow road and footpaths to either side of it. Take the path on the right of the road.

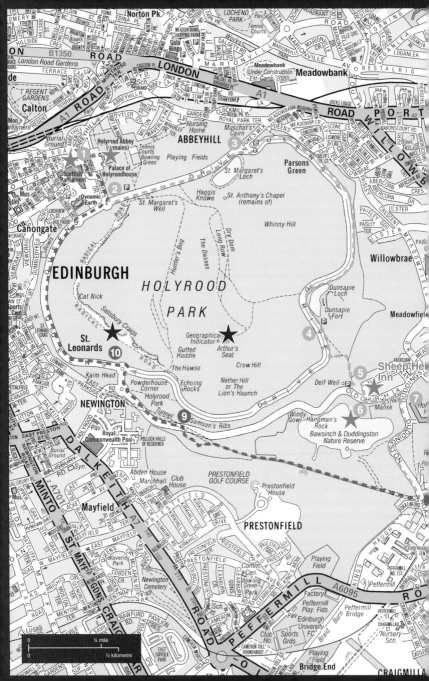

8 You are now on the old Innocent Railway route. This is indicated by a sign, but also a fingerboard here points you towards Holyrood Park. Follow this pathway as it runs almost straight for a mile (1.6 km) or so to reach a long former railway tunnel. You can see this in front of you, but just before you reach it you need to take the path on the left. This path ascends until you reach a narrow roadway crossing it, where you need to take the road to the right. Following this will lead you to a junction with a wider road, where you need to turn left and follow the path on the left of the road.

9 Continuing along here will bring you to a roundabout. The path will have moved away from the road, but by cutting through the trees on your right just before the roundabout you will see a safe crossing point. Go across here and take the right-hand turning off the roundabout. Following the path on the right of the road now, continue as the path ascends to another roundabout. The footpath passes round the far side of this roundabout and to the turn-off which leads away to the left.

10 You are now back on Queen's Drive and you can follow this road all the way round with spectacular views of Salisbury Crags ★ on your right. As the road descends the footpath switches from the right to the left of the road, and shortly afterwards you arrive at the first of two roundabouts. Cross straight over this one, then turn left at the second and you are back in Horse Wynd and can retrace your steps to the Scottish Parliament building.

ᴀᴢ walk eight

Secrets of North Edinburgh

Inverleith Road and the Ferry Road Path.

The Royal Botanic Garden is the principal destination of visitors to North Edinburgh. This walk begins from the main gates of the gardens and takes you around the surrounding area, mostly following some of the old railway paths.

Inverleith Park stands alongside the Botanic Garden. It is a popular spot for runners, but hosts many other sports too. Our walk also takes you around the pond at the southern end of the park, where the ducks and geese compete for space with the model boat enthusiasts who gather here.

We also pass Fettes College, one of Scotland's most prestigious private schools whose notable alumni include former prime minister Tony Blair, and in the fictional world, James Bond after he was expelled from Eton. The imposing main building, started in 1863, dominates the view from its surroundings.

The Ferry Road Path follows the line of a former railway, and has become something of a major conduit for North Edinburgh. At just over 1¼ miles (2.2 km) long, it is a popular way for walkers and cyclists to avoid the traffic as they cross this part of the city. Further on we join the Goldenacre Path, another of the network of former railway routes, to complete the walk.

start / finish	Royal Botanic Garden, West Entrance, Arboretum Place
nearest postcode	EH3 5NY
distance	4¾ miles / 7.5 km
time	2 hours
terrain	Mostly surfaced roads and footpaths, one unsurfaced path, some hills and steps.

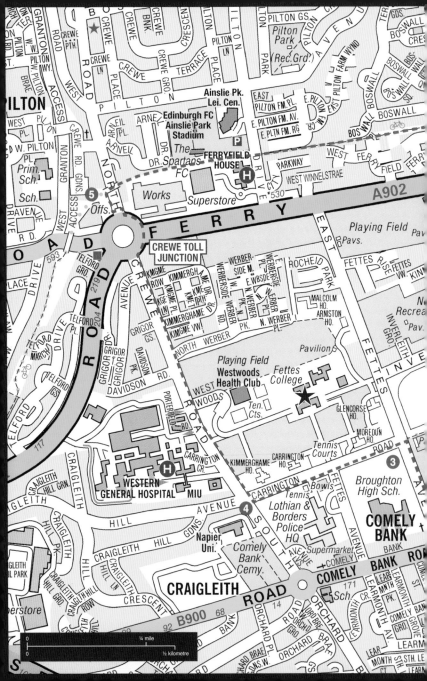

We start the walk from the West Entrance of the Royal Botanic Garden ★. To get here, there are several buses from the city centre that pass the east side of the gardens. You can either walk along Inverleith Terrace from there or through the gardens themselves, which is more pleasant. If coming by car, there is metered parking on Arboretum Place which is free at weekends.

① From the West Entrance, cross the road and go through the gates of Inverleith Park. There is a straight path ahead of you leading directly to the centre of the park where there is a stone monument. Head straight to this and then turn left and follow this path. At the other end you will come to the pond, with a path leading off on your right. Go down this path and then circle the pond, keeping it on your right.

② As you come past the end of the pond, keep going straight along the path until you reach a gate out of the park in its southwest corner. Either exit through this gate and turn left, or if you prefer, turn right and follow an unpaved path just inside the park. Either way, keep going until you reach the main western gate of the park.

③ Opposite this gate is Carrington Road. Turn left onto this and as you walk along, the grounds of Fettes College ★ are behind the fence on your right. When you reach the main gates of the college, opposite Fettes Avenue, you will have a great view of the main college building. Keep going to the end of this road and turn right onto Crewe Road South.

④ Follow this road along, noting that as you do, you get another great side view of the college building when you pass its main vehicle entrance. Keep going until you reach a large roundabout with five exits. You want to go straight on at this roundabout, so use the pedestrian crossing on Ferry Road to your right in order to do this. Turn in to Crewe Road North, cross at the pedestrian crossing, then continue towards the railway bridge ahead of you.

⑤ Go up the steps to the left of the railway bridge and turn right onto the Ferry Road Path. Continue along this path for the next 1½ miles (2.2 km). You will pass under various bridges carrying main roads and see many exits along the way signposted for the various areas of North Edinburgh.

6 Keep following the path to its end. This is a five-way junction with other paths, each marked with the name of the path itself. From left to right, the other four paths are Trinity Path, Hawthornevale Path, Chancelot Path and Goldenacre Path. It is this last one we want to take, signposted towards Goldenacre, Warriston, New Town and Centre.

7 Follow this path as it passes under Ferry Road and alongside Goldenacre playing fields. Continue until just before you are about to cross a bridge over the Water of Leith, where this path is met by the Warriston Path. You will notice a small path off to the right with a wooden fence alongside it. Take this path and it winds downwards to the riverside before veering away and heading alongside some football pitches and turning a corner into Warriston Crescent.

8 Follow Warriston Crescent to its end, then turn left and cross the bridge over the Water of Leith. Turn immediately right into Brandon Terrace using the pedestrian crossing, and stay on the right-hand side of the road. Follow the metal railing on your right until it stops and a wall begins, with a set of steps descending in between, signposted to Stockbridge and Balerno.

9 Descend these steps and follow the riverside path until it reaches a footbridge back across the river. Cross over to the Rocheid Path and turn left to continue on the riverside. Keep going on this path until you reach a gate out onto Arboretum Avenue. Turn right and ascend a short slope up to Inverleith Terrace. Cross this road, head left and then turn immediately right back into Arboretum Place. Walk straight down to return to the West Entrance of the Botanic Garden.

ᴀᴢ walk nine

Harbourside Heritage

Newhaven and its waterfront.

The port of Newhaven was constructed in the early 16th century specifically for the purpose of shipbuilding after neighbouring Leith Harbour proved unsuitable. It quickly became a popular fishing port and a centre for the landing of oysters. Today the harbour mostly hosts private leisure craft, and the old Victorian fishmarket next to it has been converted into a restaurant. The north side of the harbour also hosts a landmark lighthouse built in 1869.

Meanwhile the spit of land that juts out into the Firth of Forth beyond the harbour has mostly been developed with high-rise modern apartment blocks, but inland from the harbour you can still see some of the older cottages of the original village.

The walk also takes you through Starbank Park. Originally the grounds of a large Victorian house owned by an uncle of William Gladstone, it became a public park in the late 19th century, and its cultivated grounds command magnificent views over the Firth of Forth, making it a popular walking spot for courting couples in times gone by.

start / finish	Newhaven Harbour, Pier Place
nearest postcode	EH6 4LP
distance	2½ miles / 4 km
time	1 hour
terrain	Mostly surfaced roads and footpaths, some steep hills.

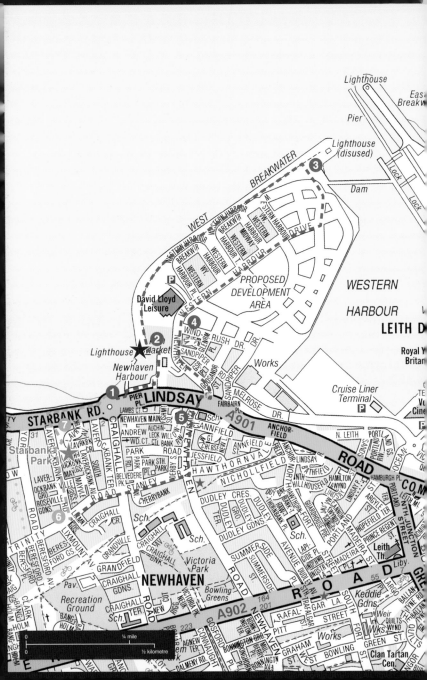

Newhaven Harbour can be reached from the city centre by bus, which sets down next to a former church. Alternatively there is on-street parking in the streets near here.

➊ From the bus shelter, walk past the harbour towards the former Victorian fish market building, which is now a restaurant. You can either use the pavement or if you prefer, descend some steps and walk along the harbour front. Just before the old fishmarket there is a set of steps on the left. Ascend these (or use the access ramp) and walk alongside the restaurant until you reach the next building, then turn left again towards the lighthouse ★ .

➋ Just before you get to the spit on which the lighthouse stands, there is a gap between a wooden and a metal fence on your right. Go through here, and follow the path along the waterfront. As you head along here, on your left you will get great views out over the Forth, and on a clear day all the way to the Forth Bridges.

➌ Keep going straight as far as you can until just before you reach the abandoned Western Harbour Lighthouse, which is fenced off. The path turns sharply right here, and then right again and joins a road near a large pond. Turn left, along this road, which then takes a turn to the right and you are on Western Harbour Drive. This is part of the modern development and there is a foot and cycle path lined with trees. Follow this all the way back towards the town.

➍ This road becomes Newhaven Place, and curves round to the left twice before taking a right turn and bringing you out onto a road junction. Use the pedestrian crossings to the left to cross over Lindsay Road. Once across, head right until you arrive at a gap in the buildings on your left with the roadsign Peacock Court.

➎ Go through this gap and on the other side is a wide street heading uphill, called Newhaven Road. Take the second turning on the right off this, onto Stanley Road. At the end of this you arrive at a four-way junction, go straight across and into East Trinity Road. Then take the second turning on the right into Laverockbank Road.

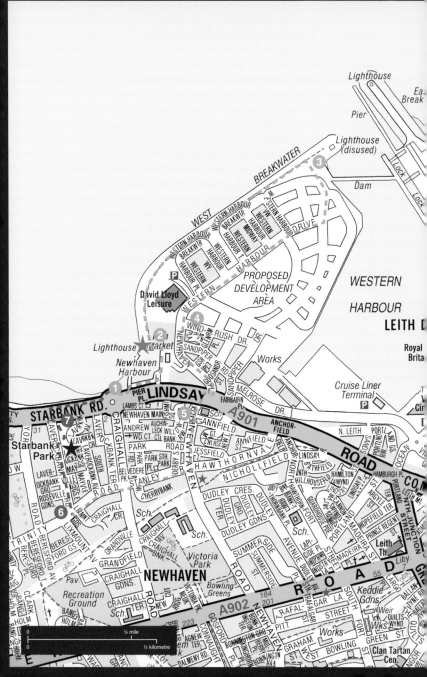

6 Continue down this road, and after crossing a slightly staggered junction, you will start to follow a stone wall on your right. Shortly you will come to a gate through this wall marked as both Starbank Park ★ and Starbank House. The house is right in front of you through the gates. Entering the park there are some beautifully landscaped gardens on your right, so if you wish you can explore these before taking the path to the left, which brings you to the top of a steep slope.

7 On the left of the slope there is a metal fence marking a pathway down. Head down here and there are various routes you can take but you want to end up at the gates at the bottom left-hand side of the park. Exit through these and cross the road, then turn right to follow the waterfront and it will bring you back to your start point. If you continue just past the start point, on your right you might notice the Harbour Inn on Fishmarket Square which makes the perfect location to finish your walk.

ᴀᴢ walk ten

Vibrant Leith

Docks and waterside splendour in the city's port.

As well as being home to the popular attractions of the Royal Yacht Britannia and nearby Ocean Terminal shopping centre, the city's port also boasts the Leith Shore, a vibrant area of bars, restaurants and nightlife. This circular walk starts at Ocean Terminal and could be combined with a visit to Britannia. It takes you around Leith's docks before we head inland along its Shore to see what else the area has to offer.

As part of the walk we follow a path alongside the Water of Leith, which reaches the sea here. We also take a wander through Victoria Park, a large area of urban parkland laid out in the early 20th century and featuring trees and flower beds, bowling greens and children's play areas. It was originally based around the grounds of Bonnington Park House, which still stands in the park.

Towards the end of the tour we pass the Leith History Mural. This impressive public artwork was created in 1986 by Tim Chalk and Paul Grime, a pair of street artists who founded an artists' collective in the area. The mural depicts the area's historic connection with the sea and was created in collaboration with a local history society to celebrate what they saw as Leith's fighting spirit.

start / finish	Ocean Terminal shopping centre, Leith
nearest postcode	EH6 6JJ
distance	4 miles / 6.5 km
time	1¾ hous
terrain	Mostly surfaced roads and footpaths, some steps.

We begin the walk from Ocean Terminal. This huge shopping centre has plenty of parking and also can be reached by bus from the city centre.

1 From the main doors of the shopping centre, turn right and walk along Ocean Drive, going straight on at the roundabout. Continue past a low wall and then before reaching the main road, turn left into an open area behind some dockland warehouses.

2 Keep going along here until you find an area with a long ornamental pond with bridges across it. Head to the far end of this pond and turn left. Follow this path round to the right where you reach a bar called Teuchter's Landing. There is an inlet from the dock here, but the bar owner has opened up a small bridge over it that is publicly accessible. Cross the bridge and follow the path until you see a large metal swing bridge on your right.

3 Cross this bridge using the footpath on the right, and at the other side, before you reach the road, turn right and almost back on yourself to follow the side of the water. This path will lead you along Leith Shore, an area of restaurants and bars, many of which are on the boats docked on your right.

4 Continue along the Shore, passing the first bridge on your right and then crossing the river at the second, signposted for Water of Leith Path. At the other side of the bridge, you will see the path itself, running alongside the river on your left. Follow this path, passing under the bridge at Great Junction Street. Shortly after this the river veers away to the left. Keep following the path.

5 Eventually the river comes alongside the path again and you will see another path turning off to the right and signposted to Victoria Park, Trinity and Newhaven. There is also a National Cycle Network marker here. Follow this path. You will pass the Stedfastgate ★, a small garden built to commemorate the centenary of the Boys' Brigade and decorated with the stone monument from the old Sinclair Fountain, moved here from Princes Street.

6 Shortly after this you pass under a green bridge and enter Victoria Park. Keep following the path you are on across the park, following signs for Newhaven and Ocean Terminal. Just before it looks like you will exit the park onto the road, there is a path to the right taking you under a blue bridge with a sign indicating that the road above is Craighall Road. Follow the path along on the other side until you come to a T junction with another path.

7 Here you need to turn right and almost back on yourself, again following a sign for Newhaven and Ocean Terminal. Continue along this path as it passes under Craighall Road again and then under Newhaven Road. A little while after this there will be a path leading to the right, again signposted for Newhaven and Ocean Terminal. Follow this path, which leads you up a set of steps and onto a road called Nichollfield.

8 Take the road directly opposite the steps, and then take the first turning on the left. At the end of this road you will see a footpath heading down the side of the last house on the left. Follow this around a corner and it comes out on North Fort Street. Turn right and follow this road until you come to its junction with Ferry Road, then turn left.

9 Walk along Ferry Road until you come to the third turning on the left, into North Junction Street. On the corner here you will find the Leith History Mural ★ on the side of the building facing you. Walk down North Junction Street until you come to the traffic lights at the end, then cross directly over this junction and it will lead you back to Ocean Terminal.

A̅Z̅ walk eleven

Leith's Bygone Times

Restalrig Railway Path and Leith Links.

Many of the networks of paths that criss-cross Edinburgh follow the lines of the city's formerly extensive Victorian railway network. The lines themselves mostly disappeared in the early 20th century, but the routes still remain and have been repurposed for joggers, cyclists and dog walkers.

Most of this walk follows the Restalrig Railway Path, which formed part of the old Caledonian Railway, built in the mid-19th century to service the docks of Leith and Granton. The path circles to the south of Leith Links before curving back round and joining up on its north side. Mostly sunken and away from traffic, it provides a pleasant countryside-feel walk in the heart of the city.

Leith itself is the main dock area of Edinburgh, and was a separate borough until it was merged into the city in 1920. The Links was once a golf course and is now its main parkland area, popular with families and those out for a stroll. It is also said to be the location where King James VII (and II of England), prior to becoming king, defeated two English courtiers at golf to settle the matter of whether it was a Scottish or English game.

start / finish	Foot of Leith Walk
nearest postcode	EH6 7AA
distance	2½ miles / 4.2 km
time	1 hour
terrain	Surfaced roads and pathways, no steep hills.

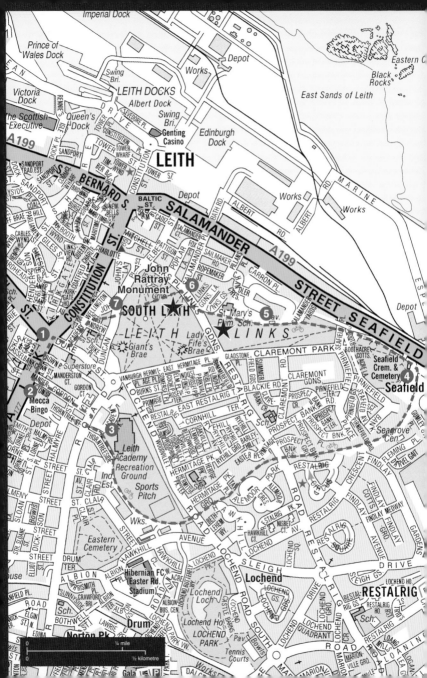

The walk begins at the foot (northern end) of Leith Walk, which is easily reached by various buses from the city centre, and by 2023 should also be on the city's tram network.

1 Starting from the junction of Leith Walk and Duke Street, follow Leith Walk in a southerly direction towards the city centre. Pass the junctions with Crown Place and Crown Street, and take the left turn into Manderson Street.

2 Follow this street along until you reach Easter Road, then cross the road and turn left. You will be passing some modern buildings on your left, and just where these end, and before the turn-off to Thorntreeside, you will see a footpath, at the end of which is a sign indicating this is Restalrig Railway Path. Turn into this footpath and follow it along.

3 A short way along you will pass two sets of metal barriers, and after this you can follow the route simply by continuing on the main path for about a mile (1.6 km). Along the way you will pass under several former railway bridges and the path is well signposted showing various destinations that can be reached from the path. Keep following in the direction of Leith Links.

4 As the path begins to curve back on itself, it begins to rise gently and you will pass Seafield Cemetery on your left. The path crosses a short bridge over the entrance to the cemetery and shortly after this crosses another bridge over Seafield Place, where it begins to descend downwards again. As you reach ground level, you will be walking along the edge of Leith Links ★, with grass parkland on your left and Seafield Bowling Club on your right.

5 Continue along this path until it joins up to the corner of Links Gardens, then continue straight on this road, crossing over to the park side of the road and following its edge. Just after Links Gardens becomes Links Place, you will see a surfaced foot and cycle path heading across the Links diagonally to the left.

6 Turn here. A short distance along you will pass the John Rattray Monument ★, a series of three vertical stones with a life-size statue of Rattray himself. A surgeon and Jacobite, Rattray won a golfing competition played on the Links in 1744 and as a result became the man to sign the original official rules of golf.

7 Continue to follow the path in a straight line as it crosses Duncan Place at a pedestrian crossing and heads back into parkland at the other side. At the opposite corner of this, join onto Acadamy Street by veering slightly left, and at the end of this road turn right to return to the foot of Leith Walk.

AZ walk twelve

Seaside Promenade

The beach and town of Portobello.

On a sunny summer day, the people of Edinburgh love to flock to Portobello to lie on the expanse of sandy beach and swim in the waters of the Firth of Forth. Three miles (4.8 km) east of the city centre, it has become a typical seaside resort with fish and chip kiosks and amusement arcades lining the promenade. But behind the seafront there are also a few things of interest to be found.

The town began as a haven for smugglers until a sailor called George Hamilton, who had fought at the siege of Porto Belo in Panama during the 18th-century War of Jenkins' Ear, decided to build a cottage here and named it after the battle. Other seamen began to build their houses nearby and the town of Portobello was born.

The town increased in popularity during the 19th century and three town halls were built in quick succession. The current town hall is the most recent, but architecturally more interesting is the second one, now a police station, designed by Robert Paterson in 1877. The walk also passes St John the Evangelist Catholic Church, an early 20th-century church built in a derivation of Gothic style, but with an unusual Expressionist tower.

start / finish	Portobello Town Hall, Portobello High Street
nearest postcode	EH15 1AJ
distance	2½ miles / 3.9 km
time	1 hour
terrain	Surfaced roads and footpaths, no steep hills.

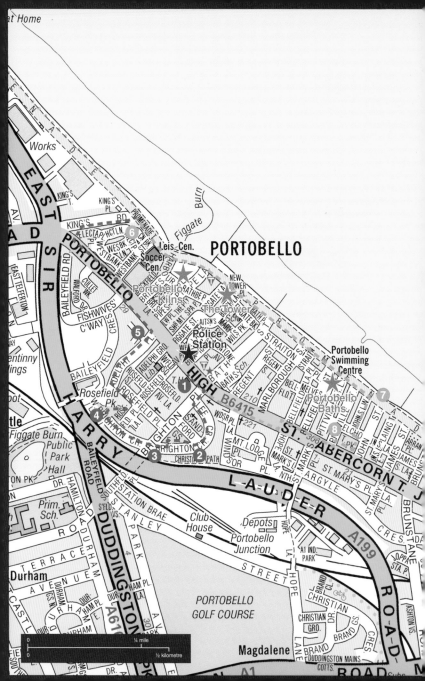

Portobello is easily reached by bus from the city centre. If you are arriving by car, there is ample car parking near the High Street.

1 Starting at the front of the Town Hall, turn right along the High Street and then right at the next corner into Brighton Place. You will see the unusual tower of St John the Evangelist Church ahead of you. Turn left before you reach it and follow Lee Crescent as it curves to the right until you reach a crossroads. Crossing over, there is an entrance to Brighton Park on your right.

2 You can continue around on East Brighton Crescent, or if you enter the park you can follow the hedge on your left until you reach another gate and exit at the next corner. From the park you will get excellent views of the church. Also, on the first Saturday of every month the Portobello Market is held in the park and is well worth a wander around.

3 At the end of East Brighton Crescent, cross directly over Brighton Place into West Brighton Crescent and continue along the road until it ends at a gate into Rosefield Park. Head through the gate and follow the path ahead of you. There is a short detour off this path to the left if you want to see the Figgate Burn, a stream around which Portobello was originally built and which winds its way through the park with wild plants on either side.

4 As you leave the park past a children's play area, ahead of you is Rosefield Avenue. Stop and look to the end of this road to get a view of the 19th-century former town hall, now the Police Station ★. However, the route takes you left out of the park, along Rosefield Place, which you follow to the end. Ahead of you, you will find a short bridge across the Figgate Burn, which affords another nice view of the stream between the houses. Cross over and turn right into Adelphi Place. This is a street of quaint old single-storey terraced cottages. You will need to turn right to continue on this street after a short distance as otherwise it ends in a cul-de-sac.

5 When you arrive back at the High Street, turn left and keep going in this direction, crossing over at a pedestrian crossing as you go. You will find yourself approaching a busy roundabout, and just before you reach it there is a footpath leading away from the road on your right. Follow this path until you come out onto King's Road, then turn right and walk down this road until you reach the seafront.

6 Turn right onto the Promenade and follow it along. Be aware that on a sunny summer day it can be quite crowded. Along the way there are a few interesting things to see behind the seafront buildings. The Portobello Kilns ★ are two early 20th-century bottle kilns that you can spot through the gaps of the buildings soon after the start of the Promenade. The Tower ★ in Figgate Lane is a three-storey house incorporating a 1785 Gothic tower that can be seen on the Beach Lane side, with the rest of the house built to the same style.

7 Shortly after passing the old Victorian swimming baths ★ you will see a lane leading off to the right called John Street Lane West. Turn and follow this lane to the top, then turn left along Elcho Terrace to reach a gate into the park on your right. Enter the park and head in either direction, skirting the edge of the park until you reach the opposite corner.

8 Exit the park onto Pittville Street. Turn left then immediately right onto Abercorn Terrace. Continue along this road and it becomes Portobello High Street, which takes you back to the starting point.

AZ walk thirteen

The Wooded Hill in the City

Corstorphine Hill and Tower.

The walk up Corstorphine Hill requires a good level of fitness as it is a steep climb. Good walking boots are recommended, and poles could be useful. The hill is one of the traditional 'seven hills of Edinburgh', and is in fact only the fourth highest, but it is mostly covered in a nature reserve which, Arthur's Seat aside, is probably the largest undeveloped area of land in the city.

Close to the summit is Corstophine Hill Tower, built in 1871 to commemorate the centenary of the birth of Sir Walter Scott. The walk takes you past the base of the tower, which is five stories high and boasts a dramatic panoramic view of the city from the top, although it is only open to the public on certain days in the summer so you will need to plan carefully if you want to experience the view.

The hill is also home to Edinburgh Zoo, so the walk can be combined with a visit. Either way, we will be passing close to the perimeter on several occasions, so don't be surprised if you hear some animal noises. Towards the end of the walk is the Rest and Be Thankful viewpoint, a spot overlooking Murrayfield Golf Course with distant views across the city to Arthur's Seat and beyond.

start / finish	Entrance to Edinburgh Zoo, Corstorphine Road
nearest postcode	EH12 6TS
distance	4 miles / 6.5 km
time	2 hours
terrain	Mostly dirt pathways, some surfaced roads, steep hills and steps.

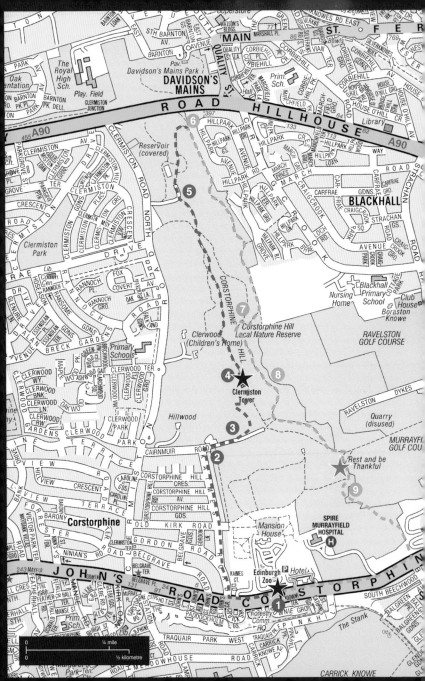

We start from the steps in front of Edinburgh Zoo. Several buses from the city centre pass here and the bus stop is just a short distance away. If coming by car, you can park at the zoo or in one of the nearby streets.

1 With your back to the zoo, turn to the right and walk along the road until you come to a right turning into Kaimes Road. Head up the road all the way to the top. It is very steep, but will gain you most of the altitude you need while using a road with a paved surface.

2 At the top of the road, turn right on Cairnmuir Road, and directly ahead of you is the entrance to Corstorphine Nature Reserve. Pass to the left of the metal barrier, and walk along the path beyond. As you follow the path along on the level, you will see a low wall on your left. Just as this wall ends, a path branches away to the left, follow this and begin ascending again.

3 The path soon takes you out of the trees and into a large clearing. Follow it round to the left and you will see a waymarker for the John Muir Way. Keep going, and shortly you will see another of these with an arrow pointing to the right. Follow the arrow, and any further waymarkers, until you reach the base of Corstorphine Hill Tower (also known as Clermiston Tower) ★ .

4 After exploring the tower, look out for the first of several square concrete pillars that mark the way in these woods. There is writing on three sides. Go to the side that says 'Queensferry Road', and then walk straight ahead away from this side. You will come to some steps leading downwards, and then follow the path beyond. The path is not always clear, but this area is popular with dog walkers so the main path is generally the most trodden one. You should pass another of the concrete pillars; again follow the Queensferry Road side.

5 Eventually, after you have walked a distance of nearly ¾ mile (1.2 km) from the tower, you arrive at the end of a surfaced road which leads off both to the left and straight ahead. Take the straight-ahead road, which soon becomes a gravel track and runs along the side of a fence next to Barnton Quarry. The path is much more obvious from this point.

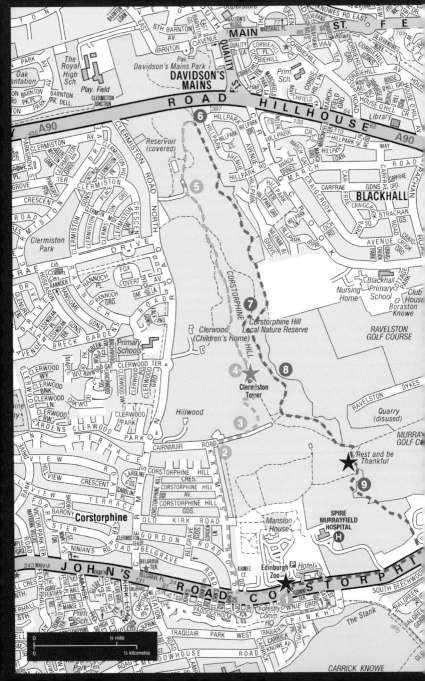

6 The path ends at a triangular junction where it is crossed by another gravel path. Turn right and follow this along, you will now find yourself walking along the lower side of the hill with the backs of houses on your left. You will pass an exit to Hillpark Grove, but continue past here along the main track. On this stretch, on a clear day you may get a view of Craigcrook Castle away to your left. Eventually this path leads to a steep set of steps leading up to the right.

7 At the top of the steps is another of the concrete pillars. On this occasion take the side that reads 'Tower' and head directly away in this direction. The path goes through the trees and veers almost immediately away to the left before passing a wooden fence. Following this you will see some green wire fencing on the left, follow the path alongside this. On the other side of the fencing is a sheer drop through the trees.

8 The path then leads to a metal fence alongside the golf course. Follow this path until you reach another path with a metal fence directly ahead of you. This fence is the perimeter of the zoo grounds, turn left and follow it as far as it takes you. You will pass the Rest and Be Thankful ★ viewpoint here, and will also notice you are once again following waymarkers for the John Muir Way.

9 The fence leads to a stone doorway. Go through here and keep following the path and the John Muir Way as it leads you downhill. This will eventually bring you to the corner of a red brick wall. Take the path to the right of the wall and it runs back down to the main road. Exiting the gate at the bottom, turn right along the road and this will return you to the front of Edinburgh Zoo.

◼⬛ walk fourteen

Riverside Meander

Cramond and the River Almond.

The River Almond essentially forms the western border of Edinburgh itself. On its eastern bank lie the suburbs of the city, to the west there is mostly open land. The first mile (1.6 km) of this walk follows the riverbank, passing quaint cottages and taking in dramatic views of the river as it winds its way down through a tree-lined valley.

The river was important during the Industrial Revolution, with water mills being used to power the factories that sprang up on its banks. We will walk past one of these, the Fair-a-Far Mill, which sits in a dramatic spot below a weir in the river.

The mill itself is now in ruins but in the 18th and 19th centuries it was a manufactory of iron tools for farming, using iron imported from Russia and Sweden. There has been a mill on this site since 1676 and the weir was constructed around 1790 to provide power for the iron works.

Away from the river we walk through some of Edinburgh's less-known parkland, and also alongside Lauriston Castle, the grounds and gardens of which are open to the public and well worth a visit.

start / finish	Junction of Queensferry Road and Cammo Road
nearest postcode	EH4 8EA
distance	4½ miles / 7.25 km
time	1 hour 45 minutes
terrain	Surfaced roads and pathways, dirt pathways, some steps and steep hills.

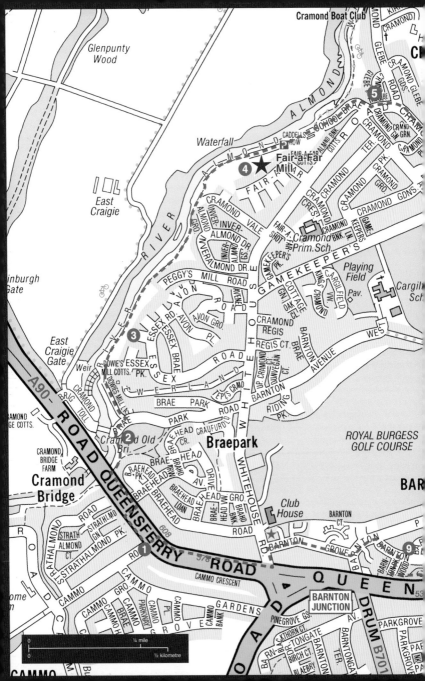

The walk begins on the A90 Queensferry Road at the junction with Cammo Road. The bus from Waverley Rail Station drops off here at the Braehead Avenue stop, or if you travel by car there is roadside parking in Cammo Road itself.

1 From Cammo Road, turn left and walk down Queensferry Road, using the pedestrian crossing to cross to the other side. Continue until you see some wooden fencing with a gate and a sign for the River Almond Walkway. Go through the gate and take the path ahead of you (not the steps to the left) and follow this path as it descends towards the river. Keep following until you reach a gate leading to a road.

2 Once through the gate, there is a bridge on the left but you need to take the road that goes ahead of you, and then almost immediately turn left at the next turning onto Dowie's Mill Lane. The road is fingerposted for River Almond Walkway and Cramond Foreshore. Shortly after the buildings in Dowie's Mill Lane end, the surfaced road becomes a narrow path, and there is a wooden fingerpost pointing through the trees labelled 'Cramond'. You can either follow the signpost or continue on the path you are on; both routes join up again shortly, but going through the trees gives better views of the river.

3 A little further along you will come to a metal and wooden staircase with three metal gates. The riverside path ends at a cliff just after this, so you have to ascend the stairs and take the path along the top, from which you get dramatic views down to the river itself. This path ends with another staircase returning down to the riverside.

4 The path then takes you past the ruins of the Fair-a-Far Mill ★ , and shortly afterwards ends at some yellow-and-black striped gates. Passing through these gates, follow the road along a short distance, there are some steps down to the river with iron railings, followed by a small grass park enclosed in a wooden fence. Just after this, take School Brae, the road that ascends away from the river on the right, signposted 'Bus for Edinburgh'.

5 At the top of this road turn left onto Whitehouse Road and follow it as it curves right and becomes Cramond Road North. Continue until the end of this road, where it meets a junction with Gamekeeper's Road. Turn left here to continue on Cramond Road North, and when you reach a roundabout, veer right to continue on this road.

6 As the road curves right, on your left will be open fields for some distance, and then you will reach the walled grounds of Lauriston Castle ★ . If you want to explore the grounds, the entrance is a few hundred yards (300 metres) further along. After the castle entrance, continue along until you reach a mini-roundabout.

7 Take the narrow road to the right and continue along until you find a loop of road with a grass central section. At the other side of this is the entrance to Davidson's Mains Park. Enter the park and turn right to follow the path that runs parallel to the road you have just been on. Continue along until the path turns sharply left, and follow it up a slight incline until you find a turning onto another path on the right. You might notice a small finger pointer indicating this as part of the John Muir Way.

8 Turn onto this path and follow it along. You will notice further John Muir Way markers along the way. This eventually becomes a dirt path running through a strip of woodland between the main Queensferry Road on your left and housing on your right. Continue to follow the path as it crosses Barnton Park Drive. After ¼ mile (400 metres) the path veers sharply right and passes through a fenced alley between two houses.

9 At the end of the alley, go straight ahead along a short road and then turn left onto Barnton Park Crescent. This road then meets another junction at Barnton Park View, turn left again here and keep following this road for some distance as it becomes Barnton Grove. At the end, turn left again, and after a very short distance use the pedestrian crossings to turn right onto Queensferry Road. Continue back to the start point, with the option to catch the return bus at an earlier stop if you wish.

AZ walk fifteen

The Honest Toun

Musselburgh and the River Esk.

Musselburgh is a town lying just outside Edinburgh, across the border in East Lothian. Begun as a Roman settlement in 80 AD, it predates any permanent settlement in its now larger neighbour, and retained its importance as the crossing point of the River Esk on the approach to the capital from the east.

During the Middle Ages it became known as the Honest Toun, a name bestowed by the Regent of Scotland the Earl of Mar in 1332, after the people refused payment for looking after his predecessor during a long illness. Today the town clusters around the River Esk as it empties out into the Firth of Forth, and our walk concentrates on this river with its many bridges.

The walk also takes you past the Fisherrow Harbour, where in years gone by the famous Fisherrow Fishwives would gather. These women wore a uniform of distinctive striped skirts and aprons, and carried out the hard physical labour associated with the fishing industry while their husbands were out at sea. They became a close-knit community, organizing a choir as well as taking part in the first known women's golf competition in 1811. The harbour is now mostly used for leisure craft, but fishwife dolls made locally have become something of a collector's item.

start / finish	Musselburgh Library, Bridge Street, Musselburgh
nearest postcode	EH21 6AG
distance	5¼ miles / 8.4 km
time	2 hours
terrain	Mostly surfaced roads and pathways, some steps.

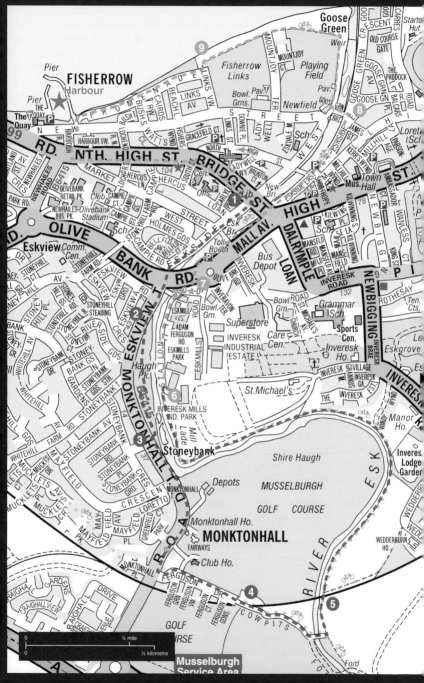

The walk starts from Musselburgh Library in Bridge Street. Buses from Edinburgh stop right outside. There is also car parking very close to here in Ladywell Way.

1 From the library, turn right to walk towards the river, then turn right onto Eskside West. Continue along the riverside, passing a footbridge over the river, until the road turns at a right angle back away from the river, and in front of you is a short footpath towards a road bridge. Follow this path which comes out next to a pedestrian crossing. Cross here and continue to follow the west bank of the river on Eskview Terrace.

2 There is a green metal fence on your left, and a short distance along, a gap in the fence leads to a path heading downwards away from the road. Descend this path into a small riverside park. Pass the basketball court and just before the children's playpark, ascend some steps on your right to reach a higher path which continues along the riverside and brings you out onto Monktonhall Terrace.

3 Continue along this road. The river turns away at a right angle to the left after a short distance, and then the road veers round to the right, passing Musselburgh Golf Club. On reaching a mini-roundabout, turn left into Ferguson Drive. Follow this along until just past the last houses there is a striped metal barrier with a footpath beyond. Pass the barrier and continue along this path.

4 The path takes you alongside the golf course and under a low railway bridge. Follow the path round until it turns sharply left and crosses a bridge over the river. At the other side it joins another riverside path. Turn left here following the signs for the River Esk Path and Musselburgh.

5 This path passes back under the railway and then alongside the river which, after a while, curves round to the left and then back to the right as you head back into the town. Just after the right turn you will pass a weir in the river and cross a small bridge over a cutting. Continue along and the path begins to run parallel to Station Road before curving up to meet it.

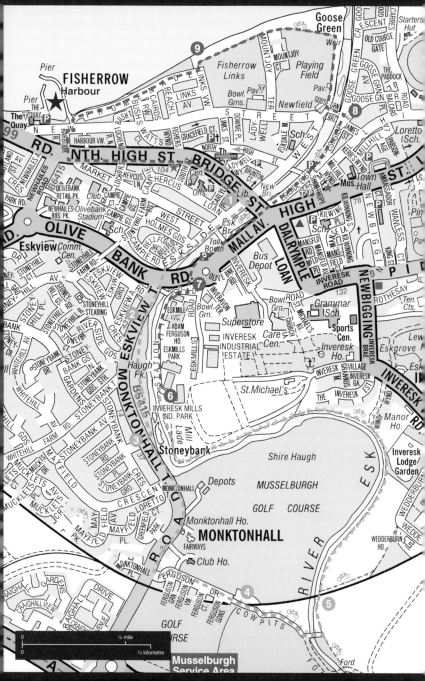

6 As you continue along Station Road you will pass a small stone marking one of the turf-cutting stations from the Musselburgh Riding of the Marches. This tradition has been carried out every 21 years since 1682 and involves dignitaries of the town processing around the ancient boundaries renewing their claim to the land by cutting a piece of turf.

7 Towards the end of Station Road you will approach a road bridge, with some steps up to it on your left. Ascend these steps and cross the road and take the riverside footpath on the other side. Continue down the riverside, passing the footbridge and going underneath the next road bridge, which is very low so mind your head. Continue along Eskside East, passing one more footbridge, until you arrive at two bridges close together. The first of these is for cyclists and the second, a metal box bridge, is for pedestrians.

8 Cross this and turn immediately right at the other side, passing a short row of houses and onto another footpath. Follow this path as it turns left around a building, then continue along until you come to a metal barrier and the path meets up with Mountjoy Terrace. Immediately around this corner, a path leads off to the right following the coastline of the Firth of Forth. Walk along this path, and if it is a clear day you will have excellent views of Arthur's Seat and even the National Monument on Calton Hill ahead of you.

9 The path zig-zags right then left as it passes the next set of buildings and eventually arrives at Fisherrow Harbour ★. Feel free to explore the harbour area for a while, then take Harbour Road, a short road that heads straight inland from the centre of the harbour. Turn left at the end and follow the road back along, past the Brunton Theatre, to return to your start point.

AZ walk sixteen

Stately Stroll

Dalmeny House and the Forth coast.

This walk takes you through the manicured grounds of Dalmeny House, a 19th-century gothic revival mansion 8 miles (13 km) west of the city centre. Home to the Earls of Rosebery, the house was built here to replace Barnbougle Castle, which you will also see nestled among the trees nearby. The current structure is an 1881 rebuild.

After passing these buildings, the walk takes in a dramatic stretch of the Firth of Forth coast before turning back inland. Along the way you will get fantastic views across to the Fife coast and back towards Edinburgh, as well as some superb views of the three Forth Bridges.

The walk starts in the village of Dalmeny itself, very close to St Cuthbert's Church which is well worth a look around. Said to be one of the most complete Norman churches in Scotland, it was built around 1130 and is largely unaltered except for the replacement tower that was built in 1937 in a sympathetic style.

start / finish	Dalmeny village cross (junction of Main Street and Bankhead Road)
nearest postcode	EH30 9TT
distance	5½ miles / 8.7 km
time	2 hours 15 minutes
terrain	Surfaced and gravel roads and pathways, some steep hills.

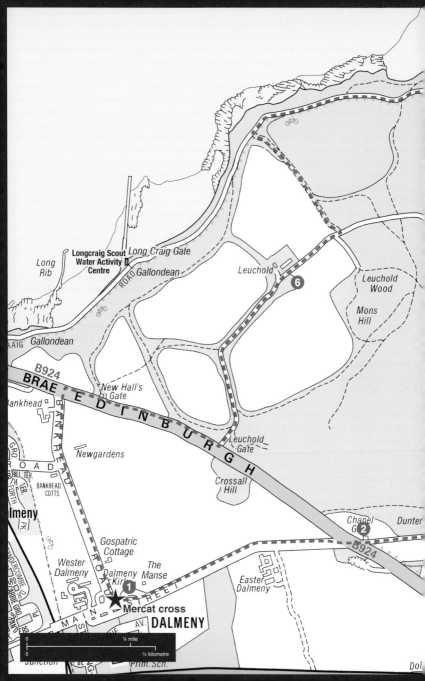

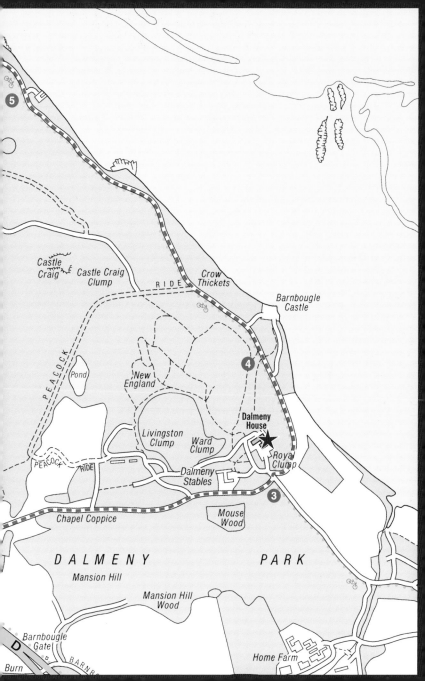

5

Castle Craig

Castle Craig Clump

R I D E

Crow Thickets

Barnbougle Castle

PEACOCK

Pond

New England

4

Livingston Clump

Ward Clump

Dalmeny House

★

Royal Clump

PEACOCK RIDE

Dalmeny Stables

3

Chapel Coppice

Mouse Wood

D A L M E N Y   P A R K

Mansion Hill

Mansion Hill Wood

Barnbougle Gate

D

BARNB

Burn

Home Farm

The village of Dalmeny can be reached from Edinburgh on the Queensferry bus. Alight the bus as it turns at the village cross. Alternatively, if coming by car, pass the cross and you will find roadside parking further into the village.

1 From the mercat cross, turn left along Main Street, past St Cuthbert's Church. Follow the footpath to the left of the road out of the village until you reach a junction with the B924 road, which you need to cross. Facing you is an entrance to the grounds of Dalmeny House. There is an automatic gate across the road, but a pedestrian entrance on the left-hand side of this.

2 Go through the entrance and walk along the road. Note that there is no footpath here and vehicles do use this road, so you may have to step onto the grass at the side when they pass. Try to keep to the left-hand side. As you continue along this road you will pass several outbuildings and gardens, but keep going straight on until you arrive at Dalmeny House ★ itself.

3 As you come in sight of the house, the road splits in several directions. Take the second of these on the right, signposted for Barnbougle Castle, and this takes you around to the right-hand side of the house. Be aware that you are walking through a golf course, so be wary of stray balls. As you reach the edge of the golf course there is a white wooden gate with a pedestrian access on the left. Go through here and continue straight on.

4 A short distance further on you will pass the entrance to Barnbougle Castle on your right. This is not accessible to the public, but you can get views of it through the trees. Just after passing the castle, the road splits with one road leading away to the left. Keep going straight here, following the path signposted 'Fishery Cottage'. As you head along this path you will be very close to the shoreline with some excellent views out across the firth.

5 Keep going, passing Fishery Cottage on your right, and shortly afterwards the path veers sharply left. Follow it on round and keep on this path as it passes through woodland with occasional views of the firth, until you reach a junction with a surfaced road on your left. Take this turning. The road quickly becomes a gravel surface again and then climbs steeply uphill. At its top it arrives at another surfaced road, turn right here and as you pass along this stretch you will get amazing views of the Forth Bridges on your right.

6 Shortly after this you will pass a vermouth distillery with some interesting topiary outside. Continue to follow the road as it turns left and heads downhill, until you reach a white gate with a pedestrian access on the right. Go through here and onto the main road, and turn right. Follow this road until you reach a turning on the left signposted for Dalmeny. Turn and follow this road and it will take you back to your start point.

AZ walk seventeen

The Three Bridges

South Queensferry and the Firth of Forth.

Crossing the Firth of Forth 10 miles (16 km) northeast of the city centre, the three Forth Bridges are among the most iconic images of Scotland. The distinctive red steel Forth Bridge has been carrying trains across the estuary since 1890. Alongside it, the Forth Road Bridge opened to traffic in 1964, with a second road crossing, the Queensferry Crossing, opening a little further upstream in 2017. This walk can be completed as three distance options, all of which include great views of the bridges.

The walk takes you around the town of South Queensferry whose name, along with that of its counterpart North Queensferry on the opposite side of the Firth of Forth, derives from these being the termini of a ferry service across the estuary established by Queen Margaret in the 11th century, which operated until 1964.

We also pass along the quaint, narrow High Street, at the beginning of which is the 17th-century Hawes Inn, which features in Robert Louis Stephenson's *Kidnapped*. Further along we pass the Jubilee Clock Tower, originally built in the early 18th century but remodelled in 1887 for Queen Victoria's Golden Jubilee.

start / finish	The Loan bus stop, South Queensferry
nearest postcode	EH30 9SD
distance	Short walk – 2 miles / 3.4 km
	Medium walk – 2¾ miles / 4.5 km
	Long walk – 4 miles / 6.3 km
time	45 minutes, 1 hour or 1 hour 30 minutes
terrain	Surfaced and gravel roads and pathways, some steep hills and steps to climb.

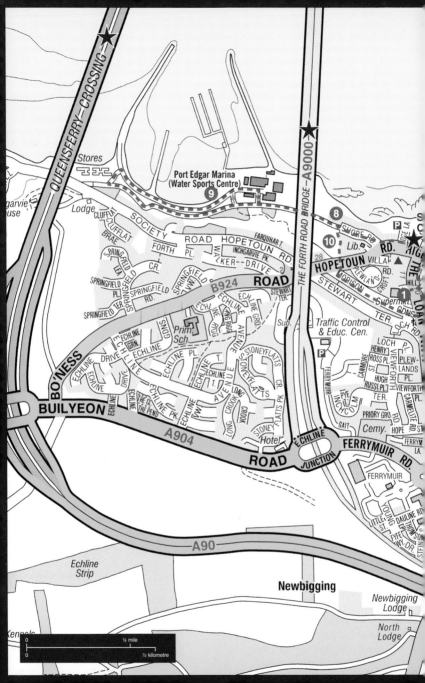

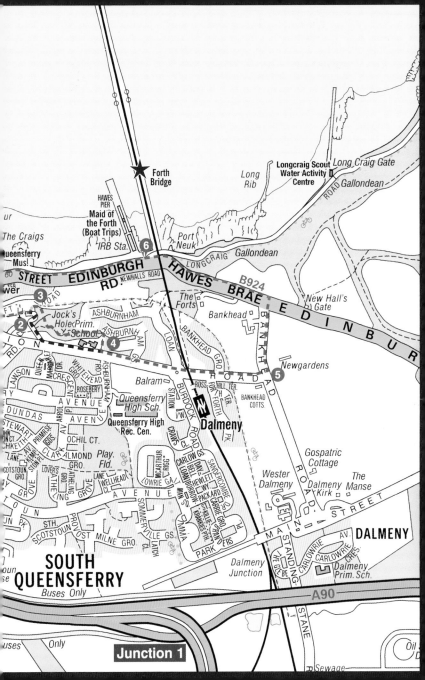

Forth Bridge

Longcraig Scout Water Activity Centre

Long Craig Gate

Gallondean

Long Rib

Long Rib

HAWES PIER

Maid of the Forth (Boat Trips)

IRB Sta.

The Craigs

Queensferry Mus!

Port Neuk

Gallondean

LONGCRAIG

6

B924

ROAD

STREET EDINBURGH RD. HAWES BRAE EDINBUR

NEWHALLS ROAD

3

New Hall's Gate

The Forts

2

Jock's Hole Prim. School

ASHBURNHAM

Bankhead

BANKHEAD GRO.

BANKHEAD

ASHBURNHAM

ASHBURNHAM GR.

4

LOAN

ROAD

Newgardens

5

Balram

ROSS

HILL TER.

FOR'TH TER.

HILL PK.

LAWSON

QUEEN MARGARET DR.

WHITEHEAD GRO.

ROSEBERY CT.

ARROL AV.

ASHBURNHAM GR.

STATION

BANKHEAD COTTS.

DUNDAS

AVENUE

AV

CRESCENT

BURDOCK

ROAD

Queensferry High Sch.

Queensferry High Rec. Cen.

Dalmeny

STEWART

JOHN CT.

INCHKEITH AV.

CLARK

OCHIL CT.

ALMOND GRO.

PRIMROSE GDS.

KEMP STON PL.

LOVERS' LANE

ATHELING 'NG

Play. Fld.

LANE

WELLHEAD

CRAWS

VW.

CARLOW GS.

OAK ...

BEL HEWLETT

LOMBROW

ST. KILLIE

WY

PACKARD

SANDERCOMBE GS.

CARRIE GRO.

FRANKLIN PTH.

Gospatric Cottage

The Manse

ROAD

Wester Dalmeny

Dalmeny Kirk

SCOTSTOUN GRO.

GRO

SCOTSTOUN

STH.

PROVOST

SOMMERVILLE GS.

MILNE GRO.

MCARTHUR

LOWRIE GA.

AVENUE

PARK

ANDERS

HG GR. BE

MAIN

STANDING

CARLOWRIE AV.

CARLOWRIE CRES.

STREET

DALMENY

Dalmeny Prim. Sch.

SOUTH QUEENSFERRY

Buses Only

Dalmeny Junction

STANE

Only

A90

Buses

Only

Oil S

Sewage

Junction 1

The walk begins at the bus stop outside the large supermarket on The Loan in South Queensferry, which is served by buses from the city centre. If coming by car, there is a pay car park at The Binks, down at the bottom of this road, but be aware that it is quite small and fills up quickly so arrive early. Alternatively there is on-street parking, but you may need to drive around for a while to find a space.

1 Heading up The Loan you will see Queensferry Parish Church on the left of the road, and just before you reach it, a footpath branches away to the left, opposite the entrance to Morison Gardens on the right. Turn along this path, signposted for Dalmeny Station, and follow it along, where you will notice another path following the same line some distance below you on your left. Also to the left you will get the first of several great views of the bridges.

2 Keep following this path until just after you pass the entrance to Station Road Park. You will notice a path leading away into the wooded area on your left, with a noticeboard at the entrance announcing this as Ferry Glen. If you want to avoid walking on rough dirt paths, continue straight on until you reach the road and turn left. Otherwise, turn and take the path through the trees. These two routes will join up again later.

3 If you head through the trees, the path descends towards a bridge across a stream, and then rises again at the other side, following this stream until at the top there is another bridge crossing on your right. Follow this and it will bring you out onto the main road, next to St Margaret's Primary School. Turn left and you will be following the same road as those who took the easier route.

4 Continue following Station Road until you reach a mini-roundabout next to the railway station. Cross straight over and pass under the railway bridge, then continue along to the end of this road. You will cross a bridge with a footpath underneath, this is the lower path you saw earlier. At the end of the road you will reach a junction with Bankhead Road. Cross to the other side where there is a footpath and turn left.

5 Follow this to the next junction where you will again have to cross to reach the pavement, and turn left heading down the hill. This quite steep hill passes between some trees and as you near the bottom you will pass underneath the Forth Rail Bridge ★. You can hear the rumble and feel the vibrations if a train passes along the bridge while you are under it here.

6 From here keep straight on to pass along the High Street, also called Newhalls Road. Initially the view is open to the Forth on your right, and then you begin to pass between buildings. Just after you pass the Jubilee Clock Tower ★ there is a turning on the left. This is The Loan, if you wish to take the short version of the walk, turn here and it will take you directly back to the start point.

7 Otherwise keep straight, passing St Mary's Episcopal Church ★, the only medieval Carmelite church still in use in Britain. You will reach a fork where the main road veers left. Take the right fork here and keep going until just before you are about to pass under the Forth Road Bridge ★. On your left you will notice a gap in the wall with steps leading up through it. This is the route to take if you are following the medium-length walk, in which case jump to step 10.

8 For the longer walk, keep going straight and pass under the bridge. You will soon come to a barrier in the road with a wooden hut next to it. Pass the barrier on the right and keep going. You will come to where the road turns right and there is an access through a fence ahead of you. Pass through this and keep walking along a

vehicle-width paved path. Follow this as it keeps going, with trees on your left and boatyards on your right. You will have excellent views of the Queensferry Crossing ★ all the way along. Eventually you come to a point where the path is blocked by fences. Turn right here and go down onto Shore Road to come back along through the boatyards themselves.

9 You will eventually arrive at the Marina buildings, with a bar called Down The Hatch on your right. Keep going into the car park ahead and then follow the main route as it turns right. This brings you back to the road under the bridge. Retrace your steps until you find the gap in the wall with the steps again, and then turn right and go up these.

10 Heading up through the trees you will come to an open grassy area. Follow the footpath round to the left and you will see a path branch off to the right in front of a stone bridge. Turn here, pass under the bridge and follow the footpath on the other side as it rises to join Morison Terrace. Keep going along this road and you will come out opposite Queensferry Parish Church with your start point down the hill on your left.

▣Z walk eighteen

House of Former Glory

Lasswade and Mavisbank House.

Lasswade is a small and picturesque village sitting in Edinburgh's commuter belt, 6¼ miles (10 km) southeast of the city centre. It nestles in a valley between the more modern developed towns of Bonnyrigg and Loanhead. The village has become something of a retirement community and is dotted with impressive old houses, connected by a twisty warren of small roads and pathways.

From the village, this walk leads you along the bank of the River North Esk to Mavisbank House, a derelict mansion whose current condition belies its significance. The house was designed by the celebrated architect William Adam and was the first villa in Scotland to be designed in the Palladian style, with building work beginning in 1723.

Sadly, years of neglect and a fire in 1973 have left it in an unstable condition and currently it is only viewable through high fencing. There are tentative plans to partially renovate the property with a view to opening it as a community asset. It was one of the properties featured in the BBC television series *Restoration* in 2003, in which the public voted on a restoration project to fund, but ultimately was not chosen.

start / finish	The Laird and Dog Inn, High Street, Lasswade
nearest postcode	EH18 1NA
distance	3¼ miles / 5.3 km
time	1 hour 15 minutes
terrain	Surfaced roads and dirt pathways, some steep hills and steps.

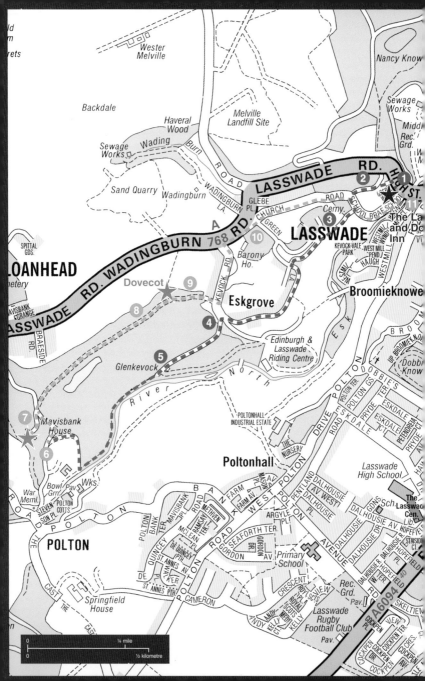

Lasswade can be reached by bus from the centre of Edinburgh, which stops near The Laird and Dog Inn. If you are travelling by car, there is a small free car park by the Lasswade Pavilion, round the corner from here. After parking, go past the war memorial and across a footbridge and this brings you directly to the pub.

1 Facing The Laird and Dog Inn ★, you will see the pub car park on the right, and just past it is a wall with a narrow path to the right of it, leading away from the road. Follow this path which heads steeply upwards and comes out on a road next to a monument to Richard Baird Smith, former Chief Engineer of Delhi, who was born here.

2 Follow along this road, which passes between a cemetery and the ruins of the 13th-century Lasswade Old Kirk, and emerges out of a gate opposite some ornate gates to another part of the cemetery. Turn left, and go a short distance downhill until the cemetery wall ends and you see another footpath with a metal barrier at the end, signposted for Polton. Follow this footpath.

3 As you go along this path there are some excellent views over Lasswade on your left. The path ends at another road, and across from you there is a wooden sign simply reading 'Footpath' and pointing to the other side of the gates to a large house. Follow this path until you reach some wooden barriers where the path forks at the other side. Take the right-hand fork and it will lead you through some more barriers and eventually down to a complicated road junction.

4 Across from you, you should see another set of metal barriers and a narrow footpath leading steeply downwards. Follow this path through the woods until you come to a wooden gate with a 'North Esk Way' marker and a signpost reading 'Alternative path to Mavisbank House and Polton'. Go through the gate and follow the well-defined path on the opposite side, which goes directly to the left.

5 After a while you will come to a metal gate with a wooden gate to the left with another North Esk Way marker. Go through the wooden gate and you will find yourself following the riverbank. In the distance you will see a circular walled garden. Just before you reach this, there is a short path on the right leading to a wooden gate, signposted 'Mavisbank House'. Go through this gate and follow the path on the other side as it takes you round to the right of the walled garden.

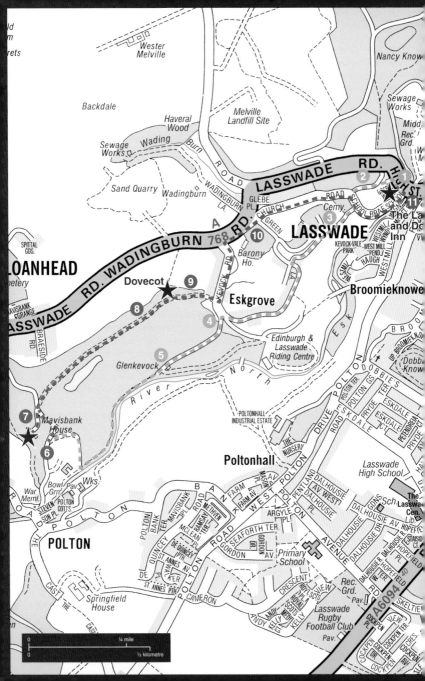

6 At the opposite side of this garden, the path turns back on itself, again signposted for 'Mavisbank House'. Follow this path, which leads uphill then curves to the left at the top. There is a grass turning on the left as you curve round, ignore this one then go left at the next corner, turning diagonally back on yourself. This path leads to the front of Mavisbank House ★ itself. The house is derelict so you can only view it from the outside through the fence.

7 Once you have finished viewing the house, retrace your steps along the path. Ahead of you, you will see a metal farm gate, and to the right shortly before it a wooden access gate in the fence. Go through this wooden gate and there is a visible if not well-defined path on the other side. Follow this path, being careful as water drains into a lake to your right here, and so even in summer the path can sometimes be sticky with some boggy patches.

8 Keep following this path until you reach a fork with a caution sign in between the two paths. Take the left fork here, and keep following the path. Towards its end, if you look up to your left you will see the ruins of a 1738 dovecot ★ , originally built as an eyecatcher at the end of the landscaped grounds of Mavisbank House.

9 Just past this you come to a metal farm-type gate, and on the other side a patch of grass leading to a paved driveway. Go through the gate, being careful to close it behind you, and cross the grass to the driveway and out to Kevock Road. Turn left and follow the road along to where it veers left and then joins the main Wadingburn Road. Turn right onto this road.

10 A short distance along you will see a turn to the right, leading to a narrow one-track road with 20 mph signs at the end. Turn onto this road, which is Church Road. Keep following it along. You will cross your earlier path after a while, going between the Old Kirk and the cemetery. On this occasion, instead of turning off, follow the road down the hill as it becomes School Brae and curves to the left to follow the riverside.

11 Shortly afterwards you will come to a road bridge across the river. Turn left and it will bring you back to The Laird and Dog Inn where you began the walk. You can catch the bus back to the city (or return to your car) here, or you may wish to stop for refreshments.

▲Z walk nineteen

Ancient History in a Modern Town

Eskbank and Newbattle in Dalkeith.

Newbattle Abbey was an important Cistercian Abbey founded in 1140 under the patronage of King David I of Scotland. It became a favourite with subsequent Scottish kings, many of whom visited and became generous benefactors. Situated in the picturesque valley of the River South Esk, 8 miles (12.7 km) southeast of the city centre, the abbey was converted into a stately home following the Reformation, and the buildings later became a college.

Our walk passes the gates of the abbey with fantastic views of the building itself. If the gates are open, feel free to walk up the driveway for a closer view of the building or to take photos. The house itself can be hired out as a party or wedding venue and guided tours of the property are possible if booked in advance.

Newbattle Parish Church, also known as the Old Kirk, stands nearby on a site that has been occupied by a church since the founding of the abbey. The current church was built in the 1720s after the medieval church had fallen into disrepair.

The walk also passes the Newbattle Viaduct. Dating from 1849, it was built to carry the main line between Edinburgh and Carlisle across the River South Esk. It was closed to passenger traffic due to the Beeching cuts in 1969 but was reopened in 2015 to carry the Borders Railway from Edinburgh to Tweedbank.

start / finish	Eskbank Railway Station, off Dalhousie Road
nearest postcode	EH22 3NA
distance	2¾ miles / 4.4 km
time	1 hour
terrain	Surfaced roads and dirt pathways.

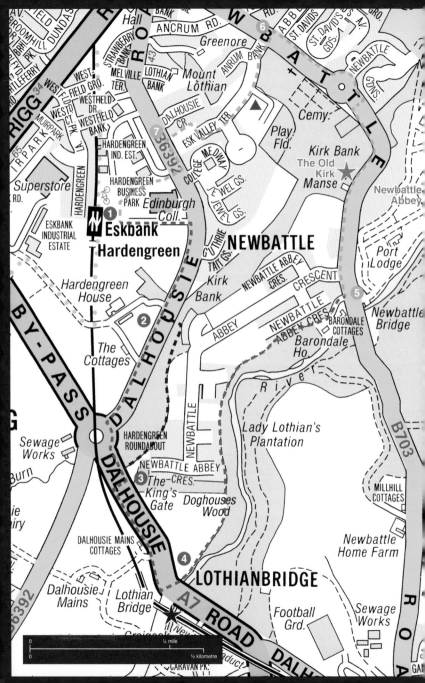

The walk begins at Eskbank railway station, which is a 20-minute train ride from Waverley with trains running regularly. There is a large free car park at the station if you prefer to drive, and the bus from the city stops nearby if you would prefer to arrive this way.

1 From the station, walk through the car park and past the Edinburgh College campus on your left, until you reach Dalhousie Road. Turn right along this road.

2 You have the option to continue along this road to the roundabout and, using the traffic islands to cross carefully, take the first exit from the roundabout, heading left. Alternatively, after passing the speed limit signs on Dalhousie Road, look out for a footpath on the left, signposted to Eskbank. If you wish, you can take this path through the woods until it comes out into some grassland behind a modern housing development. Cross the grass to the road here, turn right and right again, and at the end of this road you will see a narrow path alongside a fence that will lead you to an arched gate back onto the main road. If you use this route, turn left out of the gate to be on the same road as above.

3 Walking up this road, just past the bus shelter you will have to cross to the other side to continue on the footpath. Be careful, this is the main A7 road and can be busy. Keep going as the road curves to the right and ahead of you is the Newbattle Viaduct (known locally as Lothianbridge Viaduct) ★ looming above the road. Just as you reach the first arches of the viaduct, you will see a footpath signposted 'Newbattle' leading away to the left of the road just before it crosses a bridge over the river. Cross carefully again and follow this footpath.

4 The footpath leads you alongside the River South Esk. It branches at various points, but all of the paths lead to the same place so feel free to take whichever route you wish. The leftmost route is the easiest walking, but routes on the right have better views of the river. All of the routes lead to a gravel track running past the quaint Barondale Cottages and towards the main road where you emerge next to a set of buildings with a clocktower at the rear.

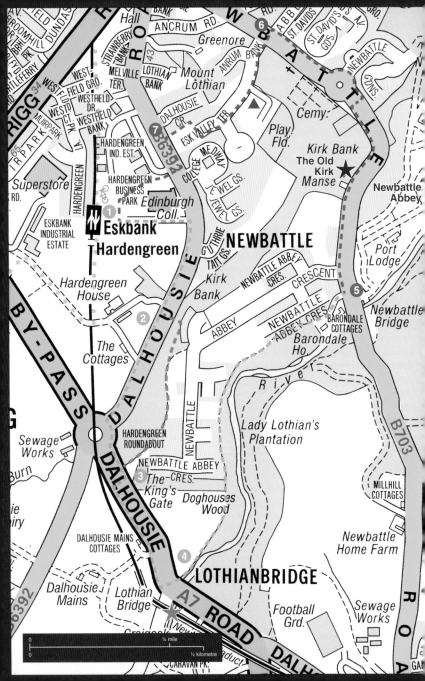

5 Turn left here and you will soon see the gates of Newbattle Abbey ★ itself on your right. If you would like to explore the grounds, feel free to do so, then return to the road to continue the walk. Keep going along the road, between two stone walls, and shortly you pass the early 17th-century Newbattle House, followed by the Old Kirk ★ . The road curves left and uphill after this, and you will need to cross it when the pavement comes to an end. Go straight over at the mini-roundabout and continue along the road past a cemetery on your left.

6 Cross back over the main road at the traffic lights and turn left into Ancrum Bank, continuing on as it becomes Esk Valley Terrace. At the end of the road, turn right and in front of you, you will see a footpath that curves round to the left. Follow this and it will bring you to Dalhousie Road.

7 Turn left onto the road and walk up until you come to a pedestrian crossing. Cross over, and directly ahead there is a foot and cycle path signposted for Eskbank Station. Follow this as it runs around to the rear of Edinburgh College, and you will return to your starting point.

AZ walk twenty

Beyond Rosslyn Chapel

Roslin Glen Country Park.

With its unique architecture and connection to Dan Brown's *The Da Vinci Code*, Rosslyn Chapel is one of the most popular day-trip destinations for holidaymakers to Edinburgh. However, not all visitors who make the 7½-mile (12-km) journey south from the city spend time exploring the chapel's surroundings and discovering how much Roslin Glen Country Park also has to offer.

Just a stone's throw from the chapel is Roslin Castle, an imposing ruin sitting atop a rock outcrop with a dramatic bridge access. Originally built in the late 14th century, the current castle dates from the mid-16th, the previous one having been destroyed during the War of the Rough Wooing. Only the outer courtyard can be visited by the public, the restored East Range now being used as holiday accommodation.

The walk also takes you through the site of the old Roslin Glen Gunpowder Mill. While little of the factory itself remains, you will pass through the ruins of some of its water mills, and an information board displays a plan of the old factory to help you understand what you are seeing.

start / finish	Rosslyn Chapel car park, Chapel Loan, Roslin
nearest postcode	EH25 9PU
distance	3 miles / 5 km
time	1 hour 15 minutes
terrain	Surfaced roads and dirt pathways, some steep hills and steps.

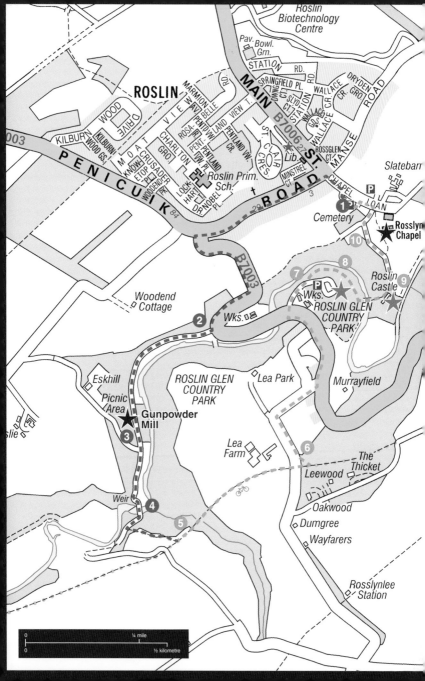

The village of Roslin can be reached by bus from the city centre. This stops on Main Street, from which the chapel car park is a short walk. If you are arriving by car and planning to visit the chapel itself, park in the dedicated car park where the walk starts. Alternatively, free parking is available at Roslin Glen Country Park on the B7003; if parking here, start the walk at step 7 and jump back to the beginning of the instructions when you reach the chapel car park.

1 From the chapel car park, walk away from the chapel and towards the village. When you reach the top of the road, turn left into Penicuik Road. Follow this along until you come to a turning on the left signposted to Rosslynlee Hospital and Roslin Glen Country Park. Turn down this road, which almost immediately curves to the left and back on itself. Keep following this road as it winds steeply downhill and bends round to the right twice. There is no pavement, so care is needed, especially on the blind corners.

2 You will reach the place where the road turns very sharply left and back on itself. At this point, ahead of you are the gates to the gunpowder mill ★, with a large wooden sign next to them. Go through these gates and follow the path on the other side. As you walk along this stretch of path you may notice large recesses cut into the hillside on your right. These are where buildings of the gunpowder mill stood. They were built in these recesses so that, if an accident caused an explosion, the blast would be directed away from the other surrounding buildings.

3 After passing the main factory site the path forks, with one path staying up high and the other descending steps to the riverside. Either path will lead you to the same place, but the left-hand path will take you through the mill buildings. At the other side of the mill buildings you come to a bridge across the river.

4 Cross the bridge and at the other side the path splits again, with the right-hand path staying on the level. Take the left-hand path, which rises up some low steps and is signposted for Penicuik to Dalkieth Walkway and Kirkettle. Keep going up this path until you reach a wooden gate at the top, after which you descend some steps to meet a surfaced pathway.

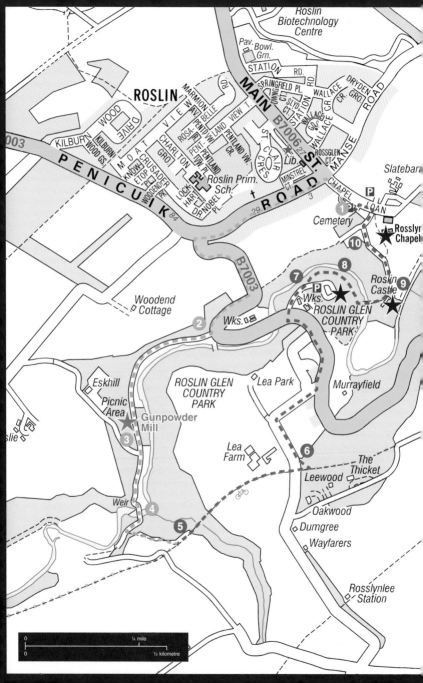

5 Turn left here, signposted for Roslynlee Car Park, Rosewell, Bonnyrigg and Dalkeith. Follow this path along until it is about to pass under a bridge, with an old disused railway platform on your left. Ascend onto this platform and continue along under the bridge. A signpost down below you on the right indicates a path to Roslin Glen Country Park and Rosslyn Chapel and Castle. Follow this path as it leaves the platform on your left, then turns back behind a low brick wall and ascends to a surfaced road.

6 Once you reach the road, turn right and descend the hill. After a while the road turns right at a right angle; keep following it until you reach a T junction. Turn left here, still following signs for Roslin Glen Country Park ★. As you walk along you will reach an entranceway with a wooden sign reading 'Roslin Glen'. Turn right into here and walk towards the car park.

7 If you parked here this is where you start and finish the walk. On the drive between the road and the car park, a path leads off to the left signposted 'Rosslyn Chapel and Castle, Polton and Springfield Mill'. Follow this path for a good riverside view, or just go straight on through the car park if you prefer.

8 The path will bring you out in the picnic area, and as you continue to follow it, and any signs as above, you will find a bridge across the river. Cross this, and at the other side turn left and ascend the hill where the path curves to the right and up some low steps. As you ascend, the steps become steeper, and on your right you will get views of Roslin Castle ★ through the trees, and then of the bridge that crosses to it.

9 At the top of the path, you can turn back on yourself and through some gates to cross the bridge to the castle. Be aware that the wall is quite low and there are sheer drops on both sides, so if you are afraid of heights it might not be a good idea to cross. Once you have visited the castle, retrace your steps back across the access bridge and go straight ahead. The path now leads you between two graveyards, and to a junction.

10 Take the path to the right, signposted simply 'Roslin'. At the top of this path, the Rosslyn Chapel car park is on your left. If you are visiting the chapel ★, the visitor centre is on your right.

images